Pictorial Reflections of Herefordshire Cricket

by

Ken Hook and Frank Bennett

see
p. 53/54

Enjoy the read!

Ken Hook

Frank Bennett

To Fres / for all her kindness

Gordon

Gordon

1

Published by Impact Print & Design Ltd.
Impact House,
Coldnose Road,
Rotherwas,
Hereford
HR2 6JL

First Published by Impact Print & Design Ltd. 2009

ISBN : 978-0-9561136-1-0

Printed in Great Britain by
Impact Print & Design Ltd, Hereford

Contents

Pictorial Reflections of Herefordshire Cricket

Acknowledgments

Peter Manders, Ricardo Ellcock, Jack Bannister, Patrick Murphy, the late Joff Leng, Ian Jackson, Barry Grubutt, Jose Middleton, Martin Bentham, Clare Burton-Edwards, Carol Roberts, Tim Jones, Paul Notley, Rex Roff, Les Gibson, Nick Osborne, Roy Wargen, David Essenhigh, Ivor Lloyd, John Evans, Mick Harmon, the late Jim Finney, Steven Bishop, Alan Hartland, Andy Morris, Derrick Jones, Peter Sykes, Tim Lowe, Derek Foxton, Derek Watkins, Bob Reynolds, Jim Sandford, the late John Taylor, Trevor Jones, Dr. Julian Wheeler, Bryan Smith, Robin Hill, John Chadd, Derek Hince, Ernie Morgan, Roger Pye, Peter Burgoyne, Gordon & the late Elaine Lamputt, Colleen Rogers, Brian Messam, Bill Masefield, Roy Smith David Hodges, Doc Lewis, Simon Dent, Alan Roberts, Cliff Davies, Bill Jackson, Stewart Blyth, Michael Scudamore, Jim Clarke, Kath Mawson, John Gummery, Godfrey Davies, Tom Morgan, Marian Campbell, Nigel Yarwood, Cedric & Anne Davies, Marsha Davies, Margaret Noakes, Michael Best, Gerald Bishop, Adrian Berry, John Eisel, Keith Bishop, Brian Smart, the late Francis Perkins, Douglas Lloyd, Norman Williams, the late Ernie Smith, Trevor Watkins, Margaret Lewis, Alec Haines, Keith Edwards, Frank Reynolds, Allan Edwards, John Hall, Keith & Roberta Hodnett, the late Anne Sandford, Nigel Davies, Les James, Stan Marston, George Warley, Neville Sandford, Geoff Morris, Jane Cawley, Richard Prime, Ray Norton, Jock Thompson, John Gurney, Ray & Sheila Hince, Richard Hope, Jake Morgan, Len Sparrow, Harold Gurney, Malcolm Hughes, Stephen Davies, Richard Sparey, Michael Best, Mike Tidmarsh, Gordon Wood, Sadie Cole, Ray Cooper, Beryl Staite, Dick Davies, Tony Jones, Alan May, Brian Goode, Cath Mawson, Dennis Gwatkin, Chris Moore, Howard Sharp, Ian Robinson, Mick Carroll, Tim Ward, Liz Hughes.

Introduction

Pictorial Reflections of Herefordshire Cricket

The authors Ken Hook and Frank Bennett decided to produce this book because of the substantial amount of material, especially photographs, that was left over because of lack of space following the publication of *Cricket in Herefordshire in the 20th Century*.

That book was so well received by the cricket lovers of Herefordshire and beyond, that it was decided by the authors to research many more special situations that have occurred.

Many cricketing personalities who have lived or have had a connection with the County have also been referred to.

Many Hereford companies have been generous sponsors of Herefordshire cricket during the present and last century and it was felt appropriate to pay them a tribute.

The early days of cricket are included to inform younger readers about the important beginnings of cricket, cricket grounds and distinguished people.

Tribute has been paid to some personalities who have had a substantial influence on cricket in the County and who have sadly passed away.

Cricket has always had its humorous side and this is captured in the cartoons and caricatures.

For many of the local sides the highlight of their season have been the tours that they undertook, and this has been dealt with in another chapter.

Once again the ladies and youth who take part in this great game in various forms are included.

Cricket in Herefordshire in the 20th Century included numerous photographs and anecdotes from former cricketers and their families. Hundreds of names of players were included under the various photographs, and there were inevitably some discrepancies and omissions caused by the dimming of memory and passage of time. Some of those amendments were brought to the attention of the authors and on the basis that it was felt that many readers of the first book would be reading *Pictorial Reflections* a section has been added to show appropriate alterations

The authors sincerely hope the cricketing fraternity of our County and beyond enjoy this book as much as the first one.

Ken Hook & Frank Bennett

Foreword by Damien D'Oliviera
On behalf of **Basil D'Oliviera**

It gives me great pleasure to write a few words on behalf of my father and myself as a forward to Ken and Frank's new book *Pictorial Reflections of Herefordshire Cricket*. Many hours of research have ended with a great achievement in writing this historic cricket book, which many other counties do not have.

I know my father Basil spent many happy hours in Herefordshire either turning out for his own benefit matches or those of his Worcester colleagues over the years. He recalls with affection games at Hereford, Ross, Bromyard and Kington. He also enjoyed many evenings participating in end of season presentation dinners and made many after dinner speeches at clubs such as Leominster, Almeley and Canon Frome. Although my father is not in the best of health at present I know he will enjoy being involved with this book as he and Ken shared the odd pint of beer at New Road on a few occasions.

I have had quite a lot to do with Herefordshire cricket and cricketers as a coach with Worcestershire CCC. Players coming for trials and also when playing for Worcestershire with former Herefordshire players such as Rueben Spiring and Steve Watkins. In recent times I have been involved with the set up of a Worcestershire CCC Satellite Academy in Herefordshire for players aged 14 to 16 to act as a feeder Academy to our main Worcestershire Academy, and have worked with players like Ben Stebbings and Sebastian Warwick as well as a very good working relationship with Steve Williams and Ed Price. Both are excellent coaches with player development at the top of their agenda.

Basil and Damian D'Oliviera
by the authors

Basil Lewis D'Oliveira CBE was born on 4th October 1931 in Cape Town South Africa. During the early days he became captain of the South African non-white cricket team.

He emigrated to England with help from John Arlott the cricket commentator in 1960, and joined Worcestershire County Cricket Club in 1964. He became a British citizen in 1966.

Basil's international career with England also started in 1966, and in 1967 he was the Wisden Cricketer of the Year. During his career with England he played in 44 test matches and scored 5 centuries with a batting average of 40. He took 47 test wickets as a medium pace change bowler. He was awarded the CBE for his services to cricket in 2005.

Basil's son Damian was also born in Cape Town on 19th October 1960, and followed in his father's footsteps by joining Worcestershire County Cricket Club. He played first class cricket with Worcestershire from 1982 to 1995.

He is a coach with Worcestershire and is now the Academy director. The authors thank Damian for his invaluable co-operation with the forward to this book.

Ken Hook and Frank Bennett

The Authors

Ken Hook and Frank Bennett are local men both with a keen interest in cricket and local history. *Pictorial Reflections of Herefordshire Cricket* is the second book they have written together, the first was *Cricket in Herefordshire in the 20th Century* which was published in 2007.

Ken played cricket in the county for 30 years and was an active administrator for the clubs that he was involved with.

Frank has been a cricket enthusiast all his life and is a supporter of Worcestershire. He is a long standing member of the Hereford Musical Theatre Company.

CHAPTER I

Early and Local History

In this the opening chapter the authors have endeavoured to find interesting facts and accompanying photographs about cricket in general and in particular individuals and situations that are connected with Herefordshire.

Above: Lords Umpires Cufflinks.

Below: Association of Cricket Umpires badge which both belonged to the late Phil Noakes, who was Chairman of the Herefordshire Umpires' Association and jointly, with another local umpire, Harry Miles, officiated in the Prudential World Cup Series in 1968.

Thomas Lord, a proud Yorkshire man from Leeds, was born in November 1755 and became a founder member of Marylebone Cricket Club in 1787. The Marylebone ground was moved on two occasions and each time the wicket was dug up and transferred to the new setting. The present 'Lords Cricket Ground' is the result of the second move. Herefordshire Cricket has a proud connection with the ground. Herefordshire County Club played at Lords in the year 2000 and won the E.C.B. 38 Minor Counties Cup beating Cheshire in the final. In 1993 Kington Cricket Club went to Lords and won the National Village Knockout Competition.

Left: **Dr. W. G. Grace** came to Hereford in May 1890 with a Gloucestershire 12 who played an 18 from Herefordshire captained by Lord Chesterfield. Grace is the gentleman with the full beard; Lord Chesterfield is sitting on his right. The match was played at Wyeside, the ground of the Hereford Cathedral School, but due to atrocious weather the game finished as a rain affected draw.

Who said they were the good old days?
Hurrah for the helmet!

On the 17th May 1895 a banquet was held to commemorate W.G. Grace's
100th century.

Umpiring signals: from left to right: four runs; leg bye; wide;
out; no ball; one short and a bye.

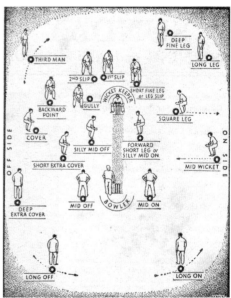

Popular orthodox field placing, assuming a right
hand batsman and a right arm bowler.

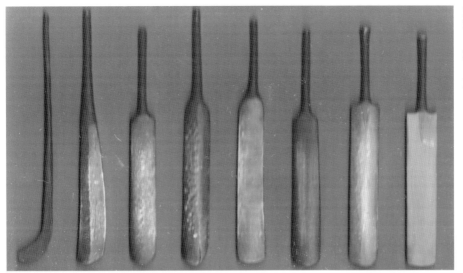

History of the Cricket Bat
Left to right: Early Curved 1720; Curved Bat 1750; Early Straight 1774; Little Joey 1792; E. Bagot 1793; Fuller Pilch's 1835; W G Grace 1901; Jack Hobbs 1930.

CRICKETERS' INN.

HENRY BENTLEY,

WIDEMARSH WITHOUT, HEREFORD,

Embraces this favourable opportunity of returning thanks to the Gentlemen visiting his Cricket Ground, and to the Public in general, for the patronage he has received during the time that he has occupied the above house, and hopes, by supplying good articles at reasonable charges, to merit a continuance of that support.

CRICKET BAT & STUMP MANUFACTURER

To Lord's Cricket Ground, and to the Principal Clubs in England.

H. BENTLEY,

CRICKETERS' INN, WIDEMARSH WITHOUT

HEREFORD,

Begs respectfully to inform his Friends that they can be supplied with warranted Articles, of well-seasoned materials and of the most finished manufacture. Orders by post promptly attended to.

GOODS WARRANTED FOR A MONTH.

An 1847 advert for cricket equipment for sale by the Landlord of the Cricketers Inn Widemarsh Common, Hereford.

Reg Perks, the Hereford born England opening bowler, coaching Oliver Andrews from Bringsty cricket club.

Hereford Cathedral School 1st XI 1908

Back Row L to R: G.L. Cazalet, B.R. Streeton, H.R. Ragg, Mr Shepherd (Club Professional), L.H. Shelton, R. Palethorpe.

Front Row: B.W.V. King, G.W. Grasett, W.R. Burrough (Capt) A. Watkins, H. Sharpley.

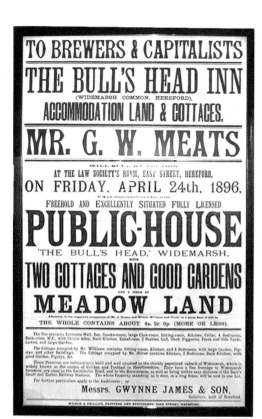

Bosbury cricket team were playing at the beginning of the 20th century. The photo confirms that there was also a ladies team in 1909.
Photo: Luke Tilley & Son Ledbury

G.W. Meats Hampstead XI 1914.

G.W. Meats *(below centre, with bat)* practised as an auctioneer in Hereford. The sale brochure *(left)* dated 1896 shows the sale of the Bulls Head Inn in Hereford. Meats clearly used his cricketing background when preparing his particular of sale because he describes the property as being "situated in the thickly populated suburb of Widemarsh, which is widely known as the home of cricket in Herefordshire."

A postcard showing Clyde House School, as it might have been when Jack Sharpe was being educated there.

Jack Sharpe *(above)* was arguably the most successful sportsman born in Hereford, playing first class cricket and football. He went to Clyde House School, Edgar Street, Hereford where he was taught to play cricket by Mr E Baker and developed into a fine batsman. He played cricket for Herefordshire before moving on to play first class cricket for Lancashire and three test matches for England all against Australia in 1909. In the third test at the Oval he scored 109 and took 3 wickets.

He also played football for Hereford Thistle, Aston Villa, Everton and England. Whilst with Everton he won an F.A. Cup winners and runners up medal before becoming a director of the club. The above photograph captures him unusually showing off his bowling action.

Keith Edwards, a local builder who played cricket in Hereford for many years had the honour to mount the commemorative plaque at Eign Gate to respect Jack's achievements.

The Late Sir Paul Getty

Sir Paul Getty was the patron of Herefordshire County Cricket Club and a supporter of local cricket. He invited a Herefordshire local cricket team to play on his estate each year because of his love for the County. He was also a close friend of Brian Johnson of Test match special fame who lived at Much Marcle in the 1920s.

Peter Sykes was presented with a replica 'Old Father Time' Lords weather vane, in recognition of his services to sport on his retirement as secretary of the Hereford and District League after 26 years. Peter continues as secretary of the Herefordshire Minor Counties Cricket Club.

Hereford Racecourse Cricket Ground
The photograph shows the racecourse ground being prepared in 1908 when Hereford Cricket Club moved from Widemarsh Common.

The opening game was played on the 1st May 1909 between H.D. Leveson Gower's XI and H.K. Foster's XI. Some notable cricketers of the time took part in addition to the two Captains. Leveson Gower's XI included two County players, J.N. Crawford from Surrey and J.W. Douglas from Leicestershire. H.K. Foster, who was then Captain of Worcestershire, included in his team G.W. Grasett and the Rev A. E. Green Price. Two local cricketers, Leveson Gower and H.K. Foster, were in the same Oxford University side with H.A. Arkwright, P.F. Warner, and C.B. Fry in 1895.

Panoramic photograph of the Racecourse Ground before the 2nd World War
Worcestershire County Cricket Club played five first class matches on the Racecourse between 1919 & 1983; they also hosted the H.K. Foster XI against an Australian Imperial Forces XI in 1919.

Worcestershire County Cricket Club 1905
Back Row: E Arnold, R Pearson, F Bowley, D Smith, F Wheldon, G Wilson.
Middle Row: G Gaukrodger, A W Isaac, P H Foley (Secretary), H K Foster (Captain),
E Bromley Martin.
Front Row: ? Keene, A Bird.

P.H. Foley was a member of the Foley family from Stoke Edith. H K Foster, who was Captain at the time, later became Captain of Herefordshire and also an England Selector. George Wheldon played football for Aston Villa during the late 1900s when the side was extremely successful. Douglas Smith later became a successful sportsman in South Africa. A W Isaac was to lose his life in the First World War.

Falcons Touring Team
The Cricket Club was a team of Quakers and are known to have toured the county most of years between 1904 and 1974.

The photo is from a postcard dated 1907 and shows the team at Ledbury.
The squad were:
J. F. & W.H. Rowlands, S. & B. Priestman, W.B. L.J. & L.C. Barber, F. Neild, A.L. Stapleton, A.G. Pickard, W. Dixon, J.P. Whitlow, J.E. Pontefract and T.A. Twyman.

In 1939 The Falcons played a Herefordshire XI and beat them by 84 runs.

Hereford Gents -v- Shrewsbury Gents.

Match played at Shrewsbury School in the 1990s. This traditionally followed the example set by amateur gentleman in the early part of the 20th century including the Thorneycrofts, Foleys and other landed gentry. In latter years the team has been made up of invited local cricketers.

Ross Gents circa 1900

Photograph taken at Ross Cricket Ground in front of the original 19th Century pavilion.

Fawley Station

Cricketers have utilised many different forms of transport to travel to away matches the following are just a small sample…

1. Train & Trap

Recorded in the Brockhampton cricket club minute book for 1897. Paid for horse and trap to Perrystone 2/-(10p), Fawley station 1/6d (7.5p) and railway fare to Ross 8d (3.5p). Fawley Station has long since disappeared. The postcard *(above)* shows the Station in its heyday.

2. The Coach

Jack Howells from Brockhampton recalled that in 1930 'we used to have a coach all the way back then from Hereford Motor Co, it cost us about 6d each player for local matches'.

3. The Van

In 1945 Mr. Clay from Brockhampton offered the club one of his vehicles called 'the van' for away matches. Players were charged 1/- (5p) each for the journey.

4. A Bedford Lorry

Eric Hudson from Brockhampton remembered travelling to a match in 1945 in a Bedford lorry with an open tailboard when unfortunately someone fell out of the back. He did not recall the nature of the injuries to the unfortunate man.

5. Motor Bike

John Edwards recalled a close call after a Brockhampton game when he was trying to get back from the Farmers Boy Pub at Longhope to the Gurney's Oak Inn before closing time. Gerald Howells was on the back of the bike. They both came off at Lea near Ross directly in front of a bus, fortunately suffering only cuts and bruises. Alas the biggest upset was missing last orders! In another incident John had Ted Rogers on the back and Cecil Lilly perched precariously on the petrol tank. Cecil not surprisingly lost his nerve, put his foot on the ground and all three ended up in a heap in a hedge.

6. The Jeep

Bert Howells from Brockhampton recalled an occasion in the 1950s when he went to a cup final in Ross sitting on bales of hay on a trailer pulled by a jeep.

7. Estate Car

In 1960 Richard Phillips crammed the other members of the Brockhampton team into his estate car for an away game at Withington. Surprisingly after they had unfolded their limbs they went out and won the game.

8. Lorry

Dave Sharland recalled that in the 1930s he travelled with the Wormelow team with his father Bert to away matches in a lorry supplied by their President Mrs. Amy Symmonds.

9. Tractor & Trailer

Ivor Hunt from Canon Frome drove a tractor and trailer to local away matches with the whole team on board.

10. Bicycle

The most common form of transport for many players especially up to and including the 1960s, was the push bike, which usually went on automatic pilot to the pub after the game.

11. Armoured Car

In the 1960s Robin Warden who played for Callow Wayfarers and was also a member of the Shropshire Yeomanry TA, organised a procession of armoured jeeps from Moreton camp HQ to transport the team to Moreton and Lyde cricket ground. This was to be a form of friendly intimidation as they were placed around the ground in strategic positions.

12. Lorry

Roger Pye recalled an occasion when John Edwards (Park Farm) drove the Staunton-on-Arrow cricket team in his lorry to play at Tenbury Wells. On the way he unfortunately ran over a duck, which resulted in obvious comments from the players. John got his second duck of the day in the match, and on the way home they nicknamed him two ducks Edwards.

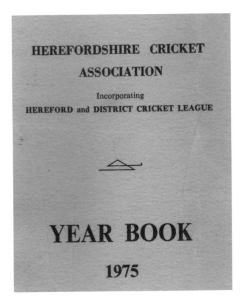

Herefordshie Cricket Association first year
book 1975

Hereford Evening League 50th Anniversary year book 1977

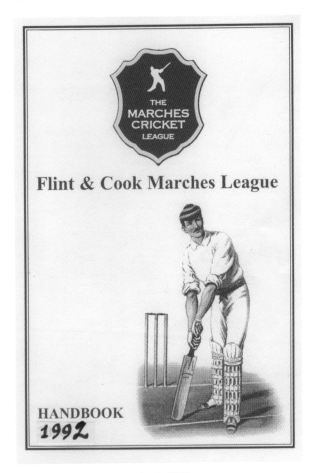

Marches League first year book 1992

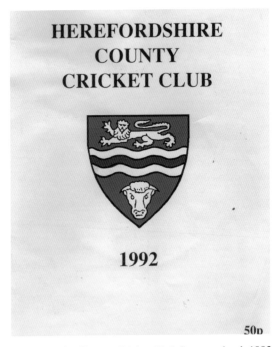

Herefordshire County Cricket Club first year book 1992

Hereford Cricket Society was founded in 1997 by local cricket enthusiasts Tim Lowe and Bob Hall, to enable members to meet and talk about cricket on a monthly basis during the winter, and to invite first class cricketers and personalities to speak to the club.

These are the guest speakers of the Society since the publication of *Cricket in Herefordshire in the 20th Century.*

2005/06: Tony Cottey, Jack Simmons, Jeremy Lloyd, Neal Radford and John Barclay.
2006/07: Stephen Chalke, Henry Olonga, Tim Roberts, David Shepherd, Peter Hayter, Matthew Engel & Clive Dickinson.
2007/08: Jason Gallian, Dennis Amiss, Mark Alleyne, Andy Lloyd, and Vikram Solanki.
2008/09: Ken Taylor, Basher Hassan, Bill Frindall, and Charles Colville.

The venue for these evenings moved from the Conservative Club to Arte in St Owens Street in 2008.

Cricket Society logo designed and drawn by Peter Manders

Bill Frindall *(below)* came to Hereford for the first time in 1958 during his national service, which he spent at RAF Credenhill. He returned to Hereford with a friend in the 1980s to show him the Mappa Mundi. During the visit he saw a house in the Tupsley area and made it his base. On moving to Hereford he played some cricket at Brockhampton, which he remembered affectionately. Bill joined the illustrious test match special team in 1966, which he still belonged to until he died of Legionnaires disease on the 29th January 2009 at the age of 69. He covered more than 350 test matches during his career and enjoyed working with his colleagues immensely.

On the 21st January 2009 Bill was guest of Honour to the Hereford Cricket Society when they were treated to a very enjoyable evening. He had made the journey to Hereford although not feeling at all well; he said he had caught a virus in Dubai from where he had recently returned with the test match special team. The Hereford cricket society were shocked and very sad to hear of his death.

Bill had a very full and enjoyable cricketing life. He published a large number of cricket books, which included four editions of Wisden Book of Cricket Records. He also edited Playfair Cricket Annual from 1986 and in 2004 he was appointed an MBE for his services to broadcasting and cricket.

Henry Olonga *(above)*, a former Zimbabwean cricketer, came to the Conservative Club in Hereford in 2007 to give a talk to the Hereford Cricket Society on international cricket and the internal problems in his country. Henry was an opening fast bowler who played for his country on 30 occasions over a period of seven years between 1995 and 2002. He was the first coloured man and the youngest cricketer ever to play for Zimbabwe. Towards the end of his career he had personal political problems in Zimbabwe and made a hasty retreat to Britain. Henry is also a very talented musician who has a wonderful operatic singing voice; he won a prestigious celebrity singing competition on television and has made a recording locally with the Hereford Cathedral Choir. At the end of his talk at the Conservative Club he treated the members to an impromptu rendering of Nessun Dorma.

Withington CC 1904

Withington were a thriving cricket club in the early part of the 20th century when the Dent family were very much involved. H J Dent is on the 1904 photograph; he was a fine opening bowler who played for Herefordshire against Worcester Club and Ground in 1904. Simon Dent, who plays for Cross Keys, Withington, is the great grandson of H J Dent and is in the photo in chapter 9. The other Dent family members playing are D J Dent (former Mayor of Leominster) and P Dent.

Another interesting player was the Rev A E Green-Price who also played for Herefordshire, the Hereford Gents and the Brecon Gents. The remaining members of the team are as follows: H E Stonyer, C G Bosanquet, S Corbett, W Jansey, W H Edwards, A F Goodwin, C and H Morgan, A and H Hill and C and J Davies.

This 1904 Withington postcard was sent to Colonel Cradock, Hotel Vancouver, B.C. and then sent on to his home at Castle Ryde in the Isle of Wight. The Colonel clearly had a connection with the Cricket Club at Withington because when his wife died in the Isle of Wight in 1909, he received condolences from the club.

During 1904 Withington's fixtures were Clyde House School, Mr Bosanquet's XI, Burghill, YMCA, Working Boys Home, Holme Lacy, Frome Valley, Hampton Court and Hereford Constitutional.

Dick *(left)* and **Peter Richardson**, born in Hereford, played for the Cathedral School before progressing to play for England.

Right: **Keith Miller**, the Australian test cricketer, played for Australian combined services XI versus a Hereford XI at Widemarsh Common in 1946 whilst he was stationed in Hereford. Peter Manders caught up with Keith and produced this drawing on his return to Hereford in 1953.

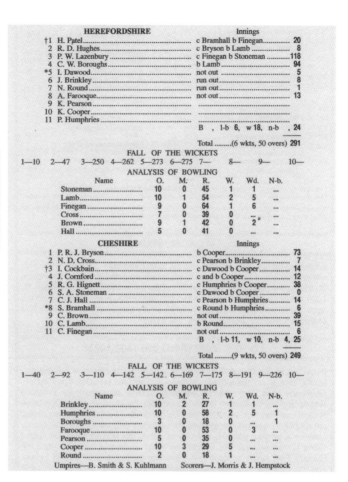

LORD'S GROUND

100th Test Match at Lord's
29th June 2000

38 COUNTY CHAMPIONSHIP – FINAL
HEREFORDSHIRE v. CHESHIRE
WEDNESDAY, 30th AUGUST, 2000   (1-day Match – 50 overs)

Scorecard of Herefordshire County Cricket Club's famous victory at Lords Cricket Ground.

HEREFORDSHIRE

	Batsman	Innings	Runs
†1	H. Patel	c Bramhall b Finegan	20
2	R. D. Hughes	c Bryson b Lamb	8
3	P. W. Lazenbury	c Finegan b Stoneman	118
4	C. W. Boroughs	b Lamb	94
*5	I. Dawood	not out	5
6	J. Brinkley	run out	8
7	N. Round	run out	1
8	A. Farooque	not out	13
9	K. Pearson		
10	K. Cooper		
11	P. Humphries		
		B , l-b 6, w 18, n-b ,	24
		Total ....(6 wkts, 50 overs)	291

FALL OF THE WICKETS
1—10 2—47 3—250 4—262 5—273 6—275 7— 8— 9— 10—

ANALYSIS OF BOWLING

Name	O.	M.	R.	W.	Wd.	N-b.
Stoneman	10	0	45	1	1	...
Lamb	10	1	54	2	5	...
Finegan	9	0	64	1	6	...
Cross	7	0	39	0		...
Brown	9	1	42	0	2*	...
Hall	5	0	41	0		...

CHESHIRE

	Batsman	Innings	Runs
1	P. R. J. Bryson	b Cooper	73
2	N. D. Cross	c Pearson b Brinkley	7
†3	I. Cockbain	c Dawood b Cooper	14
4	J. Cornford	c and b Cooper	12
5	R. G. Hignett	c Humphries b Cooper	38
6	S. A. Stoneman	c Dawood b Cooper	0
7	C. J. Hall	c Pearson b Humphries	14
*8	S. Bramhall	c Round b Humphries	6
9	C. Brown	not out	39
10	C. Lamb	b Round	15
11	C. Finegan	not out	6
		B , l-b 11, w 10, n-b 4,	25
		Total ....(9 wkts, 50 overs)	249

FALL OF THE WICKETS
1—40 2—92 3—110 4—142 5—142 6—169 7—175 8—191 9—226 10—

ANALYSIS OF BOWLING

Name	O.	M.	R.	W.	Wd.	N-b.
Brinkley	10	2	27	1	1	...
Humphries	10	0	58	2	5	1
Boroughs	3	0	18	0	...	1
Farooque	10	0	53	0	3	...
Pearson	5	0	35	0	...	...
Cooper	10	3	29	5	...	...
Round	2	0	18	1	...	...

Umpires—B. Smith & S. Kuhlmann   Scorers—J. Morris & J. Hempstock

Herefordshire players pictured on the balcony at Lords after beating Cheshire.

Herefordshire cricketers are most grateful to the many local companies who have sponsored the County's cricket during the last century.

CHAPTER II

Special Situations

There have been many interesting and unusual situations that have occurred throughout the last century relating to all aspects of local cricket.

Stuart Surridge was the former first class player for Surrey. He was Captain in the 1950s when they won the first five of their seven successive County Championships.

George and his family often entertained Stuart at their home for lunch, or occasionally they would go to the Green Dragon Hotel in Broad Street, Hereford. George retired in 1966 when he sold the business to Stuart Surridge, who then transferred everything to their base in Witham in Essex.

Left to Right: Elsie & Ralph Clarke (Son), George Clarke, Robert Clarke (Grandson), Jose Middleton (Daughter), James Middleton (Son-in-law, inset).

Above: Stewart Sturridge and George Clarke shared a joint stand at the Malvern Show.

George Clarke moved to Herefordshire from Bradford, Yorkshire. He was a manufacturer of wooden sports equipment and settled in Herefordshire in order to be close to a source of his raw material, namely ash trees. The company's first depot was at the Moorfields L.M.S. goods yard in Hereford. They then moved to Woodville House in Sutton St Nicholas in 1948. The house had many stables and outbuildings, which were converted into workshops. George personally selected his trees from the local estates, and had them cut in the round and transported to Sutton by the hauliers Harry Wraggs.

Son Ralph and son-in-law James started producing wickets and bails as a sideline but they became so popular that father George introduced them to his range. The wicket and bail business grew to the stage where they were manufacturing and packing for such companies as Slazenger, Gunn and Moor, Wisden and Stuart Surridge.

George Clarke and his Brother Willie both played for Holme Lacy Cricket Club in the mid to late 1930s. Willie was in the timber business but different from George, he formed Holme Lacy Saw Mills in the mid to late 1930s.

George's company was clearly substantial because in 1964 they co-manufactured 18,000 cricket stumps; some of them were used in Test Matches at home and abroad.

Tony Jones, an avid cricket enthusiast from Fownhope, recalled an interesting fun match played annually in May at Moorhampton Farm in the village of Abbey Dore. The hosts are the Gwatkin cider company and the match is organised by Dennis Gwatkin (director). They play under the name of 'The Flintlock Taverners'. The opposition each year is a team from Cardiff called the Welsh Cider Society organised by David Mathews. The side is made up from four small cider companies and friends. Dennis recalls wonderful days when copious amounts of complimentary Gwatkin cider was consumed throughout the day, hot dogs, beef burgers and other delicious items sizzling on the barbecue. The day is very informal and it is debatable whether the cricket or the socializing is the most important. The pitch is cut in the centre of a meadow and it has been known for sheep and cows to be there when play is in progress. The local team has not got the better of this match over the years. One year, a plan was put into action to reverse this situation. Gwatkin decided to brew a special strength cider called 'OLD STUMPER', this would surely even things up a bit! The trouble was their own players got stuck into it, and all went pear shaped and they lost again. After the match both teams retire to the farm cider house where the wives organise some good local food. Later the entertainment starts: guitar playing and much singing; it has also been known to hear the bagpipes being played in the next village. There are some interesting characters taking part including Dennis Gwatkin's brother-in-law David Stephens who plays most of the match smoking his pipe. Everybody looks forward to the next year in anticipation of another enjoyable day.

Gwatkin Flintlock Taverners team members:
Will Kilner, Alan Kay, David Buckwell, Clare Baker, Mat Baker, John Pye, Nat Jenkins, David Stephens, Kirk Painting, Paul Piejus, (front) in top hat Denis Gwatkin.

Welsh Cider Society team members. *Back row left to right: Paul, Mike, Stewart, Gavin, Andy, Fiona, Robin, Mark. Front row left to right: James, Bethan, Hywel, Dave, Jessica.*

Nosborne's Nomads, was a team run by Nick Osborne the proprietor of Pavilion Sports. During this game a superb cricket tea was organized and after the match both teams retired to the Bell Inn, Tillington to round off an enjoyable day. This photograph shows the team when they played an evening match against Burghill & Tillington circa 1990.

Standing: Bill Bowen, n/k, Len Sparrow, Adrian Price, Carl Rose, Jeremy Symonds, Vernon Jones, Derek Jones, Robin Michael, Kevin Bayliss, Nick Osborne, Paul Cook, Anthony Rivett, Alan Meredith.
Sitting: Ken Hook, Jeff Kramer, Mike Stanley, Richie Downes, Brian Symonds, Nick Price; in front with pads John Downes.

Callow Wayfarers were a team formed in 1961 at Mr and Mrs County Anderson's Callow Farm. The farm was a residential bed and breakfast establishment for professional bachelor gentlemen in the area. The team was formed in 1961 and Michael Best, a local businessman and cricket enthusiast, played a major part. The team included the eight boarders plus invited guests. Most of their fixtures were fairly local and included Harewood End, Ewyas Harold, Stoke Edith, Moreton & Lyde and the National Hunt Jockey's XI.

Back row left to right: Barry Davies, Tiger Dixon, Ivor Bloomfield, Richard Cope, David Wells, Rex Hudson.
Front row left to right: David Minear, Robin Warden, Michael Best, Roger Gates, Oscar Michell.

In 1962 Callow Wayfarers held a presentation evening at the Black Swan Inn at Much Dewchurch. The guest speaker was local national hunt jockey Michael Scudamore (sitting) who apparently said of the cricket side 'They look like cricketers until they move'!

The photograph of the dinner shows Michael Best presenting Robin Warden with the wicket-keeping prize for his unique efforts, his statistics reading: stumped 0, caught 0 and talked out 22.

Robin shot off two of his fingers in a freak accident.

Hereford Cricket Club versus Somerset, in a Bill Alley Benefit Match Sunday May 10th 1961. Bill enjoyed the match and evening celebrations too much! But, despite this, the following day he scored a century for Somerset, to the surprise of his hosts. Bill was a member of the Somerset County Cricket Club side for many years. A very young Eric Jenkins is in the forefront of the photograph.

Dick Richardson Benefit Match 1964. Played at the Racecourse.

L-R John Chadd, Tom Graveny, Bryan Smith and Basil D'Oliviera.

Ross Cricket Club invited the West Indian international cricket star Sir Learie Constantine to address their club dinner and dance in the mid 1960s. According to Rex Roff the Ross captain, it was a resounding success. The picture shows (l-r) Rex Roff; n/k; Sir Learie Constantine; JF McLean (Gloucestershire & Worcestershire until 1932; thereafter he played regularly for Ross); Mike Burrows and Mr. Birt.

Reg Perks *(second right)* at Hereford Rotary Club in 1956 was a fine first class opening bowler who was born in Hereford and played for Worcestershire and England. Len Hutton, the Yorkshire and England opening batsman, said of Reg Perks that in 1953 'he had got me out so many times that he was beginning to think of me as his rabbit'. Second from the left is a young John Chadd who went on to become captain of Hereford CC and played on two occasions for Worcestershire. He eventually became their President.

Wormelow Cricket Club were originally called Bryngwyn Cricket Club and played on a ground on the Bryngwyn Manor estate during the first decade of the 20th century. In 1965 the present club was formed at The Kennel Field and is now a very progressive club.

Wormelow Cricket Club Dinner Dance at Park Hall Ballroom in 1969, by kind permission of the owner Amos Peel. The annual dinner dance at the end of the season in the 1960s was a highlight of the season for many players and officials in local cricket when the awards for the season were presented. The photograph shows the President Dr. McGinn, who was a well-known local practitioner, with his wife, presenting the bowling cup to the clubs fixture Secretary Tony Hughes. Looking on are team member Ken Hook and Club Captain Dennis Worthing. Tony Hughes was a very enthusiastic local cricketer who tried unsuccessfully to form a Herefordshire Cricket League in the late 1960s.

 Reuben Spiring was born on the 13th November 1974 shortly after his family moved to Hereford when his footballing father Peter transferred to Hereford United. Reuben was a stylish right hand bat, who after playing local cricket signed for Worcestershire County Cricket Club. He played in 45 first class matches between 1994 and 2000, scoring 2,237 runs at an average of 32.89. The total included 4 centuries and 13 half centuries. In 1997 he won the NBC Denis Compton award. Reuben's career came to a premature end when he sustained a serious injury. He is now an aircraft pilot.

Many other local cricketers, some not born in the county and some who chose it as a later home, also achieved success in higher cricket. These include:-

Mike Hands opened the batting for Bulmers cricket club before progressing to play for Cornwall between the 1970s and the first part of the present century.

David Essenhigh started playing for Bringsty in his early teens in a team that also included his father and brothers. He then joined the MCC ground staff.

Gerald Morgan played in the Herefordshire League for Builth Wells for many years and won honours with them. He was selected to play for Wales and did so on a regular basis.

Tony Hern, who now lives at Lyonshall, played for Shropshire in the Minor Counties competition. He also played for the Burgoynes XI in the Kington knockout cup.

In 1973 **Eastnor Cricket Club** hosted a special Georgian cricket match for a scene from a film that was being shot in the area. The star of the film was actress Susannah York who is seen pictured with the cricket team, in front of the original 19th Century pavilion.

A typical departmental social cricket match played in the mid 1970s at Henry Wiggin at their Holmer ground. The team was formed by members of the Industrial Engineering Department.

Back row left to right: Cliff Farmer (department manager), Mustapha Terai, n/k, Robin Hart, Adrian Lunt, Gordon McColvin, Malcolm Hughes, John Willis, Les Collard, Joff Leng, Derek Gough.
Front row left to right: Paul Merriman, Norman Williams, Andy Williams, Roy Causon, Brian Loughman, Patrick Hughes, n/k, and Mike Shaw. In front on his own Pete Cooper. Photo by Joff Leng.

There are always some people with links to the County who contribute to cricket and are not always acknowledged locally. The following are some of these people:-

Matthew Engel lives locally and was a former editor of Wisden between 1993 and 2000. He worked on the Guardian newspaper for nearly 25 years, reporting on a wide range of political and sporting events. He is currently President of the Hereford Cricket Society. His son Laurie tragically died of cancer in 2005, aged 13, and Matthew set up a charity fund in his memory, the Laurie Engel Fund which raises money in partnership with the Teenage Cancer Trust to support patient care.

Frank Keating, who lives in the county, is a nationally known sports writer with the Guardian. He is a member of the Hereford Cricket Society and he was the first guest speaker in 1997, when the society was formed by Tim Lowe and Bob Hall for cricket enthusiasts to listen to talks by well-known cricket personalities.

Jack Bannister, the former Warwickshire opening bowler, has fond memories of Herefordshire. He was evacuated to Ross between 1939 and 1944, and lived at 28 Old Gloucester Road with the Farmer family. He recalled his memories of the Ross cricketer Rex Roff and his Father. He played his first game for Ross at the age of 13, and went on to play 374 first class matches for Warwickshire taking 1198 wickets.

Patrick Murphy was a member of the BBC Radio 3 test match special production team. He has written in the region of 30 works on cricket including The Rothmans Book of Village Cricket in which many Herefordshire teams and grounds are highlighted. Pat captained the BBC Midlands cricket team, which has played many times in Herefordshire, and since 1985 played regularly at Brockhampton. He contributed an article for the clubs 100 year anniversary book when he was pictured with G.L Clay, the President.

Pat also wrote the foreword for the Eastnor Cricket Clubs 150th anniversary booklet. Eastnor, like Brockhampton, also played the BBC team on a number of occasions, during one away match at Pebble Mill in Birmingham, the ladies were allowed into the studio to watch the making of the TV serial 'Poldark'.

Peter Manders: a self-caricature. Peter has been a prolific cartoonist of cricketers in the county for over 40 years. He has drawn individual caricatures for most of the guest speakers at the Cricket Society, which have been greatly appreciated by the speakers and members. He has provided many cartoons and sketches for inclusion in this book, for which the authors are very grateful.

Derek Evans was a well known cricket photographer in Hereford both for the local press and he also worked for national TV.

Derek Evans

F.R.P.S., F.R.S.A.

Press and Television Photographer

Richard Prime is the sports editor for the Hereford Times and is following in the footsteps of his predecessors by supporting Herefordshire cricket. Richard played cricket for Wormelow where he was captain for a number of years and also took a keen interest in the running of the club. Richard is always ready to help out leagues, clubs and individuals if they require publicity for their sporting cause.

Ted Woodriffe retired from the Hereford Times after celebrating 40 years as a sports writer in Herefordshire. Ted played some evening league cricket for the successful Gordon Lamputt XI in the 1950s. This caricature of Ted was done by well-known artist Peter Manders who was a friend and colleague on the Hereford Times.

Sports night tribute to Ted Woodriffe

at the

Moat House

Hereford

October 22

1991

Celebrating 44 years as a sports writer in Herefordshire and marking his retirement from The Hereford Times

The National Hunt Jockeys in this photo were playing in a game at Dales of Leominster. On the left is David (The Duke) Nicholson who won the Whitbread Gold Cup in 1967 on Mill House, and on retiring as a jockey he became champion trainer on two occasions. Next is M. Hamer, then comes the unmistakable Terry Biddlecombe who was champion national hunt jockey three times and as assistant trainer with Henrietta Knight who was responsible for Best Mate who won the Cheltenham gold cup on three successive occasions. The National Hunt jockeys' cricket team was formed by Michael Scudamore who was the winning jockey in the 1956 Grand National, riding Oxo. The young boy on the right of this photograph is Michael's son Peter who went on to become champion jockey eight times, and is now an assistant trainer in Herefordshire and also commentating with the racing team.

A young Peter Scudamore *(right).*

Test Match Special Team

Local cricket enthusiast, the late Joff Leng *(below right),* sent some cricket memorabilia to Brian Johnston. When Johnners responded thanking Joff, he confessed that his writing was a scrawl because he was 'inundated'.

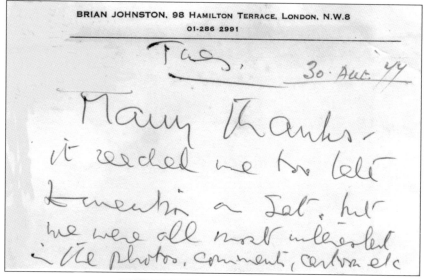

The BBC test match special team in 1989 included former local celebrity Brian (Johnners) Johnston. Brian lived at Hellens, Much Marcle in the 1920s and played local cricket in the county.

The picture shows from the top down left to right:
Christopher Martin Jenkins, Bill Frindall, Fred Trueman, Trevor Bailey, Johnners with the ceremonial cake and Henry Bloefeld.
(Cartoon by John Ireland)

Ledbury Cricket Club

1837   1987

150th Celebration Dinner
on Friday, 17th July, 1987
at The Feathers Hotel, Ledbury
7·30pm for 8·15pm
Guest Speaker: Mr. Brian Johnston
Tickets £12.50p.

Photograph of Basil D'Oliviera, the former England and Worcestershire all rounder, presenting the Fox at Bransford Six-a-Side trophy to the successful Canon Frome side.

Left to right: Brian Goode, John Evans (Club Captain), Basil D'Oliveira, Mike Sterry, Brian Cafelle, Maurice Emburey, George Whittaker.

Jim Sandford is recognized for his life commitment to cricket

Jim Sandford was honoured when he received the Rob Staite memorial trophy from Mrs. Beryl Staite. It was presented to him for his outstanding services to Herefordshire cricket. He started playing cricket for Eastnor at the age of 12. Forty-eight years later he is still playing for the same club and his ambition is to continue playing for at least 50 years. In addition to playing for Eastnor Jim also plays for the Herefordshire over 50s team. Giving something back to the game has always been a priority in Jim's life which is reflected by the fact that he has held most positions in the club at various times and is at present the chairman of ground staff.

In addition to his club commitments he has also been enthusiastically involved with county cricket. Jim helped form the Marches league in 1992 and is currently the chairman of the league. He is also chairman of the Hereford Recreation Cricket Forum as well as being on the committees of the Herefordshire County Cricket Club, the Herefordshire Cricket Board and the Worcester County Cricket League. Jim would be the first to admit that he could not give the commitment to cricket that he does without the total understanding and support of his wife Eileen, who in her own right has been involved in organizing the excellent teas at Eastnor for many years.

Derek Brimmell carries off a Lifetime Achievement Award from the Herefordshire Sports Council

Derek Brimmell has been groundsman at Colwall since 1977. He played for the team for 47 years and during this time he met many international stars including Sir Garfield Sobers, Avarinda De Silva, Tom Moody and the recently retired Worcestershire star Graeme Hick.

The Herefordshire Sports Council recently honoured him with an award for his services to cricket.

Miss Burley Gate C.C.

The picture is of **Owen Davies**, a local cricketer who went on to play for Worcestershire before the Second World War. He is presenting a bouquet of flowers to Miss Burley Gate CC in about 1958. The lovely lady is Margaret Davies (nee Symonds). Margaret, who later became a headmistress, is the daughter of Ted Symonds who was the landlord of the Moon Inn at Mordiford. This photograph was taken at the time of Owens involvement with Golden Valley Cricket club.

CHAPTER III

Touring Stories

Many local cricketers looked forward each season to their annual cricket tour. In order to make it financially easier for all members of the club to be able to go on tour, clubs would often run a standing order system, whereby the player would pay a regular amount into a fund to finance the tour.

A tour would often begin with a quick champagne breakfast at the local village pub and an early start to the journey. Before setting off the team would often put on specially designed T-shirts and load up the transport with a few bottles or cans for the journey.

After stopping off en route for a burger or bacon sandwich, it was on the road again to the hotel. Everyone would be rather tentative about the first impressions of the proprietor, especially whether or not he had a good sense of humour.

The next stop would be the first cricket ground with the team and supporters full of the appropriate 'spirit' and 'bottled' up energy. When the match was finished the serious socialising began. Participants in these tours will recall games such as the boat race, wibbley wobbley, three-man lift, fizz buzz, tip tap, spoof and the dance of the flaming backsides.

The night's entertainment did not stop at the ground, and on the return to the hotel the customary compulsory nightcap had to be consumed. Practical jokes were also the order of the day and it was not unusual for someone to retire to their room and find that there was no bed, to subsequently find it in the car park. The culprits would be the two innocent looking team members who disappeared from the bar for a short while.

The following morning would start with a large fried breakfast; the two culprits from the previous evening would be faced with a breakfast of fried food and maple syrup!! Which did not go down well on top of the previous evening's alcohol.

The frivolities of the cricket tour would be interrupted by a game of cricket and then the evening's socialising and practical jokes would start all over again. Jokes would include meat from the evenings buffet stuffed in the bedroom yale lock, and the hotel fire extinguisher being used as an oversized water pistol.

The would-be firemen who used the extinguishers would be victims the following evening with their teammates rubbing Ralgex in their underpants when they were showering.

These activities would continue for the whole week. Great fun was always had with tour fines, which often meant that the least misdemeanour was often picked up on and dealt with accordingly.

These activities always ensured that there were extra funds for repairs and damage on the club bill at the end of the week.

Leominster C.C.

Leominster Blackpool Tour in 1950. Leominster Club enjoyed a cricketing trip to Blackpool in 1950. The photo shows the team and family members waiting to get on the bus for the trip.

Left to right: Jack Bemand, Dick Burke, Dennis Parker, Mas Noden, Jim Merrett, Jack Williams, Gordon (Pokey) Powell, Stan Harvey, D.A. Davies, Uncle Bill Hall, Dennis Arrowsmith.

Blackpool ground near Stanley Park, which was the venue of Leominster touring matches.

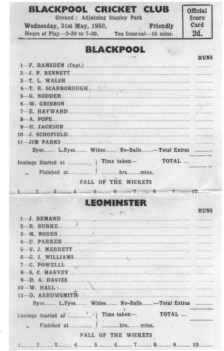

Leominster Cricket Club Blackpool tour 1950, match scorecard.

Eastnor C.C.

Smart and sober…

Richard Amott, Ray Shakeshaft, John Belbeck, Jim Sandford, Malcolm Hughes.

Before 1975 Eastnor had not been on a cricket tour, and John Taylor and Dave Entwhistle took the appropriate steps to rectify this. They went on a short holiday to the Isle of Wight with the intention of securing a base for a tour in 1976, they succeeded in finding accommodation at the Crown Hotel in Ryde. As a result the club toured the Isle of Wight for 11 years between 1976 and 1987. On these tours they played several sides including Ryde, St. Helens and the Police. John Taylor remembered the start of one tour, which was based at Warners Holiday Camp in Ryde. On arrival the tone was set when Tim Billingham was pushed fully clothed into the swimming pool. At the end of one evening one of the players tried to get into his room but his roommate, who had consumed more than sufficient drink, was snoring profusely and could not be woken. The unfortunate player spent the night in the bath. The following morning the team, feeling somewhat delicate,

made their way to the ground. They could not find the scorebook and John Taylor, who was the club's gofer, volunteered to go back to the hotel to retrieve it. When he returned some ten minutes later he found the two opening batsman fast asleep in deckchairs; the score was just three runs for four wickets down. He was then duly chastised by club Captain Jim Sandford and ordered to hurry up and get his pads on. This made John determined to succeed and he went on to score a 50, thus proving wrong the old saying: never volunteer.

On another match played at Ryde Cricket Club, Eastnor player Jim Sandford twisted his foot in a hole and was whisked off to the local Accident and Emergency department. When he returned he was in plaster up to his thigh with a suspected broken leg, which was to be checked on his return home, so unfortunately for Jim he had to sit out the rest of the tour. He was not very happy, especially when on his return home he came back from Hereford General Hospital plaster-less with no broken bones.

The tours were very popular, but John Taylor and Daisy Mayo were the only two members of the club to go on all 11 tours.

Members of the club, together with some locals from Eastnor, returned to the Isle of Wight for a reunion, remembering the locals with affection because of their hospitality.

… as the night moves on. The late John Taylor on left with Daisy Mayo, making merry.

Wormelow C.C.

Wormelow on tour to Liverpool in 1968

Back Row left to right: Handley Scudamore, Glyn Jones, Stewart Blyth, Guy Hughes, Ken Hook, Colin Edmonds.
Front Row left to right: Brian Holly, Tony M. Hughes, Dave Verry, Dennis Worthing, Alec Carter, Ralph Morgan.

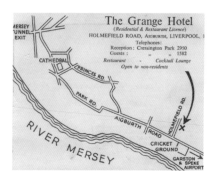

Relaxed and looking forward to facing their opponents at Liverpool are Ken Hook (padded), the late Brian Holley, Guy Hughes, Glyn Jones, and tour manager Tony Hughes. This was the first ever tour for Wormelow after they reformed in 1965. The first match was against Dunlop Sports Club at Speke in Liverpool, who, not knowing what to expect from darkest Herefordshire brought in two members of the Lancashire second XI to open the batting. Dunlop sports club batted first and hit 302 for 1 declared in 1hr 45 minutes; Wormelow had not experienced such strong opposition before. However they replied with 156 for 5, after four hours batting the club's top score to date.

On the way home they stopped off to play Harwarden in Cheshire, a game they lost, but the club found the whole experience most enthralling and for some a steep learning curve.

Goodrich C.C.

Goodrich Cricket Club have been active tourists since the 1980s. The club has visited many counties; the two photographs show memories of Hampshire and Somerset. It is interesting that the President and club umpire Eric Winchester, is present over two decades. The other tour stalwarts were Richard Hope, Mike Evans and D. Malley. Royston Young is on the New Forest photograph, and he went on to become chairman of the club. Sadly Royston died in 2007, but not before seeing the start of a new era at Goodrich, where they have recently enlarged their ground and built a new pavilion. The club have also been on tour to Liverpool, Lincoln, Pembroke, Cheddar and the Isle of Wight.

Above: Goodrich Cricket Club on tour at Exmoor in Somerset early 21st century.
Back row left to right: E. Pyatt, R. Davies, R. Friend, M. Evans, J. Frecknall.
Front row left to right: P. Evans, R. Hearth, R. Hope, A. Brown, E. Winchester (umpire), D. Malley, J. Clements.

Below: Goodrich Cricket Club on tour in the New Forest.
Back row left to right: S. Maud, S. Herbert (chairman), R. Young, P. Croudace, J. Dalton, A. Ransome, E. Pyatt, M. Watts, P. Whittaker, E. Winchester (umpire), M. Evans.
Front row left to right: M. Thompson, D. Willmott, J. Evans, D. Malley, R. Hope, I. Evans.

Burghill & Tillington C.C.

Burghill and Tillington on tour at Castle Hill Cricket Club in Kent in about 1988.

Back row left to right: Len Sparrow, Duncan Sparrow, Mike Stanley, Kevin Bayliss, Ken Hook, Alan Edge, Adrian Price, Jeremy Symonds.
Front row left to right: Paul Sparrow, Nick Osborne, Dave Mockler, Dave Parker, Brian Symonds.

Burghill and Tillington toured Kent for 20 years and formed a very close relationships with two clubs in particular Castle Hill and Staplehurst where they played every year. They also played Lynton Park, Marden, West Farley, Headcorn and Kent Dragons. During these tours they met first class and retired first class players including Derek Underwood, Alan Dixon and Brian Luckhurst, all of Kent and England and Jock Livingstone of Northants and Australia who was the managing director of Grey Nicholls cricket bats and a personal friend of Sir Don Bradman. The Burghill & Tillington players were fortunate enough to have lunch with Jock who told some wonderful stories and read a letter he had received from Sir Don discussing a recent test match.

The social side of a cricket clubs tour is nearly as important as the cricket! This photo shows the Burghill and Tillington team in full voice, singing their own version of Old Cock Robin in about 1990 whilst on tour playing Christchurch.

Burghill and Tillington invited many guest cricketers to join them on their tours including, David Parker from Golden Valley, Nick

Osborne from Ewyas Harold, Mike Hughes from Hay on Wye, Nick Nenadich from Hereford, Steve James from Builth Wells, and Phil Stock from Canon Frome.

Members of the choir are: sitting left, Len Sparrow and standing left to right Kevin Bayliss, Ken Hook, Carl Rose (partly hidden), Brian Symonds, Richie Downes and Phil Donovan, a former Lads Club and Bulmers player, who organised the tour from Bournemouth,

Pakistan Eaglets

On the 14th July 1957 Hereford Cricket Club played a match against Pakistan Eaglets on the Racecourse ground in Hereford. Included in the Eaglets team was Hanif Mohammed who later became one of Pakistans most successful players, playing for his country on 55 occasions. He was known as 'the little master' and had a career total of 12 centuries including a highest test score of 337 in 1957. and a test average of 44. In 1958 he hit 449 in a 1st class match, which was the highest individual score at the time. He was honoured as the Wisden cricketer of the year in 1968.

Well known local players are: back row 2nd right Bert Smart (scorer), 3rd right Roy Humphries (umpire), 3rd in from the right side Mike Pritchard (umpire), 3rd row 2nd right Andrew Pike, 4th right Roger Brown, 2nd row 2nd left Sir Derek Bayley, 4th left Geoff Millar, 2nd from right Ray Hill.
Front row, 3rd left Noel Pritchard, Peter Harrison front middle, Bryan Smith front second from right, John Chadd on the far right and Eric Jenkins second row 3rd from right. Hanif Mohammed is on the far left.

Colwall hosted Sri Lanka in 1979. At this time the Sri Lankan team were not as strong as now, but were able to provide strong competition for good local club sides.

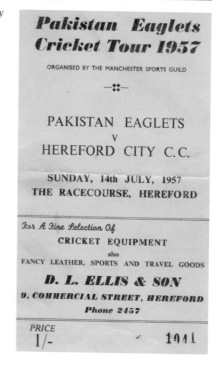

Pakistan Eaglets Cricket Tour 1957

ORGANISED BY THE MANCHESTER SPORTS GUILD

—::—

PAKISTAN EAGLETS
v
HEREFORD CITY C.C.

SUNDAY, 14th JULY, 1957
THE RACECOURSE, HEREFORD

For A Fine Selection Of
CRICKET EQUIPMENT
also
FANCY LEATHER, SPORTS AND TRAVEL GOODS

D. L. ELLIS & SON
9, COMMERCIAL STREET, HEREFORD
Phone 2457

PRICE
1/-   1941

Brockhampton C.C.

In 1988 Brockhampton made up the numbers with Bath Cricket Club to tour Australia. One of their fixtures was with the Manley Warritas who had previously toured England and played both clubs. The other clubs they played were Newcastle and Canberra. The match captured by the two photographs is against The Mayor of Manley's XI who was Joan Cooke. The one photo shows some of the players basking in the sun on the embankment waiting their turn to bat. The other photo is of Roy Wargen, of Brockhampton, talking to Max Chambers of the opposition.

Jane Cawley, the Brockhampton Secretary, recalled going on the tour. They made great friends with an Australian Max Chambers who has since been back to Herefordshire and stayed with Jane, also calling on Roy Wargen and taking in some cricket at Brockhampton. On one occasion in the mid-eighties when the Waratas toured, the club organised a fine dinner for them at the Brockhampton Court Hotel.

Brockhampton have organised many tours during the last 25 years including Essex, Devon, Cornwall, Nantwich, Oswestry and Manchester.

Cash flow was sometimes a problem and on one tour to Essex, to save money two younger team members David Best and James Price hired a transit van, in which to sleep. They also used the vehicle to transport the players to and from the grounds. Everything went well until they were ready to leave for the journey home. All the wheels had been removed from the van and the return journey was delayed until replacements were found.

On one memorable tour of St Ives the hotel was booked through an agency in Dursley and a deposit paid. However when the team arrived at the hotel no confirmation had been given and the hotel was fully booked. The proprietor of the hotel, having some sympathy with the team's situation, swiftly got on the phone and organised alternative accommodation.

The following day the team set off to play cricket, on reaching the area in which the match was to be played they came across a lovely ground which just happened to have a pub opposite. They went in, had a few drinks and ordered some food from the excellent menu. Whilst talking to the landlord about how long it would take for the food to arrive, he replied that they needn't worry, for when they want the players over they raise the club flag. All were having a good time, when about 20 minutes after they were due to start playing someone said to the landlord "they seem to be rather late with the flag". With that the landlord turned to an elderly gentleman sat on his own reading a paper who just happened to be the secretary of the club, and asked the same question. He replied "that's because we do not have a game today, you probably want the ground one mile down the road". When a player turned to the gentleman and asked "why didn't you tell us earlier?", he replied "I didn't want to interfere because the landlord was doing such a good trade".

Below: Michael Best, Brockhampton's Club Captain, meeting Tom Burns, the Australian Test umpire, who was officiating in the Manley Warritas' match.

The **Imbibers Cricket Club** is not based in Herefordshire, but the secretary was Michael Best from Fownhope. Michael Best was a long-standing player and captain of Brockhampton Cricket Club. In 1960 he organized a tour to Cornwall and booked the Red Lion Hotel at Ashburton as the clubs base. 'Screaming Lord Sutch' of the Raving Looney party ran the hotel, quite appropriately for a cricket tour, and apparently he was an excellent host. With only two weeks to go Michael had not had confirmation of the matches from his contact so he rang him just to verify matters, only to be told by his wife that he had died and nothing had been done. Michael sped down to Cornwall in his Morris 1000 and with a little charm and persuasion and the odd whisky the tour was back on track and eventually ended up a resounding success.

The following year he answered an advert in the Times and in July organized what was to be one of the first ever tours to 'Corfu'.

Hereford City Sports Club

Norman Davies was an integral part of the Hereford tours to the Caribbean.
Above: A sprightly Norman opens the bowling from the barge end whilst playing one of the "smaller" islands on the Hereford City Sports Club tour of Barbados!!!

Barbados Tours

In 1976 **John Chadd** was on a tour to Barbados with Mendip Acorns Cricket Club. He enjoyed the occasion so much that he persuaded Hereford City Sports Club to do the same tour in 1978. A committee was formed and it included, in addition to John, Norman Davies, Allan Jones and Ernie Morgan. The tour that followed was such a success that it was repeated for several years and was the highlight of many Herefordshire Cricketers' careers.

Hereford City Sports Club Barbados tour 1982 team

Back row left to right: n/k, n/k, Norman Davies, Alan Calvert, Rob Johnston, Len Sparrow.
Front row left to right: Wycliffe Phillips, Andy Hince, John Chadd, Craig Higgs, Ernie Morgan.

The photo is of the 1982 team and the two social photos are from 1981 showing the cricketing touring squad and the party ready to board the Jolly Roger for what was believed to be a wonderful trip when the odd cockspur rum was consumed!

Left opposite: Hereford City Sports club tour squad at Kensington Oval, Bridgetown, Barbados in 1981.

Members of the tour are:
Back row, 2nd from the left Charlie Layton, 3rd & 4th from the left standing are Norman Davies, Graham Burgess (Somerset), Jane Davies, far right, next to Jane at the back is Bob Brain, standing next to Jane is Paul Wright (also Somerset). 9th in the back row is Richard Bryant and from the far right Tracey Goodwin on his left John Chadd and then Tom Langford, 6th from right who later became groundsman at Worcestershire, and Graham Blomfield.

Front row, first left Wycliffe Phillips, 3rd left Virginia Chadd; next to her is Julia Goodwin and 2nd from right Nick Nedadich. The two young supporters in the front are Nicola and Jonathan Goodwin.

Kimbolton C.C.

Right: Keith Hodnett and Geoff Morris of Kimbolton on tour at Porthcawl in 1955. Keith and Geoff are the only two members of the team who are still alive; they are still great friends and have a drink together every Saturday night.

On the 3rd of August 1952, Kimbolton Cricket Club went on a tour of South Devon in a Yarrington of Eardiston coach.

The coach and driver spent the week with the team, and some of the players wives and girlfriends accompanied the players for a holiday. Keith Hodnett remembered that they stayed at the Palm Court Hotel in Torquay, which was extremely up market for a village team cricket tour. One of the teams they played was Brixham, and when they arrived everyone had fish and chips in newspaper on the beach as part of their pre-match calorie controlled preparation.

The other teams Keith remembered playing were Paignton and Babbacombe whose ground was shaped like a breakfast bowl, with the boundaries on a higher level than the pitch. After the Paignton match was over all the players had a good drink and on returning to the hotel continued the festivities with their partners. When the men went to bed they found that the ladies had tied all the legs and arms of their pyjamas, which after having had sufficient to drink proved to be quite hilarious. When they awoke the following morning feeling rather fragile, the first thing on their mind was a lovely bath to freshen up. However unbeknown to each other the men found that there was no hot water, until later when one of the girls let on that they had rammed soap tightly up the hot water taps. Roberta Hodnett hinted that the girls were made to pay for their misdemeanours although she would not elaborate! Apparently the proprietor of the hotel had a lovely clay bust of a lady on a shelf in the hall, which he obviously enjoyed very much because he took pride in pointing it out to them. On booking out of the hotel with all the niceties one does, somebody carefully placed a half smoked Woodbine cigarette end in her mouth.

Roberta Hodnett scoring for Kimbolton. Husband Keith wondering how he can get his own back for the soap trick.

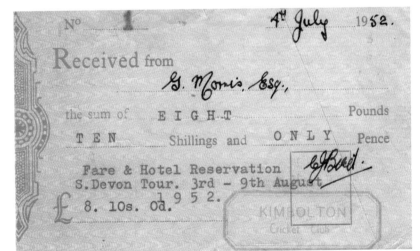

Bromyard C.C.

Bromyard Cricket Club toured Essex for a number of years; one of their members was Tony Hope a guest player from Brockhampton.

A story from one of their tours was that the late David Frost, a member of the team, was walking back to his bedroom in the early hours of the morning when he came across an open storage room. He investigated the contents and found half a dozen vacuum cleaners and as quick as a flash decided it was time for some devilment. He proceeded to plug them in all along the corridor and switch them on. When retiring to his room he heard one of the non-cricketing guests at the hotel shouting abuse at the team. Some of the team members were also awakened by the dreadful noise, and realising what had probably happened tried very hard to console the irate man. Happily the following evening the gentleman found his sense of humour and bought a couple of the players a drink and had a friendly chat with them.

On another Bromyard tour, this time to Essex, the locals were amused to witness a supermarket trolley race from the town centre to the Hotel, with a player sitting in each trolley.

Kington C.C.

Kington Cricket Club toured the Swansea area for many years during the 1970s, 80s, and 90s, and played many teams including Gowerton and Pontardulais.

Younger members of the team on their first tour were subjected to a traditional initiation: a dead octopus was put in their bed a few days into the tour, leaving a rather interesting aroma.
Kington also toured the Torquay area during the mid 1990s.

One of the members of the team was Jim Cotterell, a six-foot plus, fiery competitive opening bowler, whose image was somewhat tarnished when he received a birthday card at the hotel from 'Mummy'. When his colleagues found the card he felt like a five-foot short slow left arm bowler!!

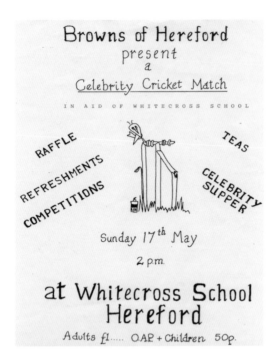

Browns of Hereford
present
a
Celebrity Cricket Match

IN AID OF WHITECROSS SCHOOL

RAFFLE
REFRESHMENTS
COMPETITIONS
TEAS
CELEBRITY SUPPER

Sunday 17th May
2 p.m.

at Whitecross School
Hereford

Adults £1..... O.AP. + Children 50p.

A short tour across the border by Worcestershire CCC players to support a Hereford charity match.

Browns of Hereford, the BMW dealer, sponsored a charity cricket match in 1987 in order to finance a new all weather wicket at Whitecross School. Many other local businesses supported Browns in this venture by advertising in the programme.

The match was played between a celebrity XI, which included a number of Worcestershire County players including the club captain Phil Neal. Worcestershire beat a Herefordshire XI in an exciting game of cricket.

Nick Osborne recalls the Hereford bowlers being under considerable attack when Ian Macklin was brought on to bowl his off breaks to try and stem the flow of runs. Phil Neal proceeded to hit him for six runs and the ball went through the school window. Phil, feeling hurt by causing damage to the property, ensured that he hit his next six clear over the school building. Roy Pienor then came in to bat and put on a batting display which was second to none to help the celebrities to victory. Roy then moved from Worcestershire to play for Kent due to their being too many overseas cricketers on the New Road staff.

Herefordshire XI:
(Umpire), Neville Symonds, Mike Rose, Terry Court, Cedric Clinkett, Ian Macklin, Jeff Kramer, Jon Cooke, Bob Binnersley, Allan Jones, Ken Watson, n/k, Simon Verry, Tracey Goodwin, n/k.

The Celebrities XI.
n/k, D Cash, Steve Rhodes (W.C.C.C.) Nick Osborne, n/k, Phil Neal (W.C.C.C. & Captain), n/k, J Brinkley, Roy Pienor (W.C.C.C. &. South Africa), John Knill (Umpire).

CHAPTER IV

Ladies

During the last century ladies have played a very important part in supporting and contributing to cricket in Herefordshire in many ways. The most obvious to any cricketer is the production of the wonderful teas. Many ladies have also donned the flannels and have played cricket to a high standard.

Below: The successful **Gordon Lamputt XI** celebrating winning Division 2 of the Hereford Evening League at a dinner dance at the Imperial Hotel in Widemarsh Street, Hereford in 1952. The side, which was founded by Gordon, had been invited to join the Hereford City Sports Club if it won the League. The photo is of the successful team with two guests dressed as cowboy and girl who were appearing at the Kemble Theatre that week.

Back row left to right: Johnny White, Alan Sheldon, Stan Kaye, Ted Rees, Les Pope, Andy Taylor, Ray Grist.
Second row left to right: Gerry Franklin, Sid Gunstone, Ros Franklin, Derek Evans, Gordon Lamputt.
Third row left to right: Mr. Bates (umpire), George Emerson.
Front row left to right: Margaret Kaye, Bernice White, Jay Gunstone, Sheila Pope, Isobel Evans, Ted Woodriffe, Elaine Lamputt, Nelson Carter, Dorothy Emerson, Betty Grist.

Twenty-five years after the 1952 celebrations Gordon & Elaine Lamputt traced as many of the original team as possible and organised an anniversary dinner at How Caple Grange in 1987.

Back row left to right: Noel Pritchard, n/k, Pat Woodriffe, Stan Kaye, Mike Pritchard, ? Carter, Johnny White, Cynthia Pole, Jimmy Pole, ? Knill, John Knill, Gerry Franklin, Arther Dawe, Ray Grist, Les Pope, Bob Delahaye.
Second row left to right: John Dewey, Ella Pritchard, Elaine Lamputt, Gordon Lamputt, Sid Gunstone, Arthur Chalkley, n/k.
Front row left to right: Derek Evans, Joan Dewey, Sheila Pope, Ted Woodriffe, Bernice White, Jay Gunstone, Priscilla?, n/k, Betty Grist.

Elaine Lamputt *(left)* with her friend Jay Gunstone. Elaine, wife of Gordon, was scorer and match manager of the Gordon Lamputt XI, which began, in the late 1940s. The team played under the Lamputt name for several years.

Theresa Warwick is Secretary of Ross Cricket Club and is also a Level One coach; it has also not been unknown for members to see her pushing the heavy roller.

In September 2007 she won an award for outstanding services to cricket from sponsors NatWest and was presented with the award at Lords. Theresa has three sons, Sebastian, Gabriel, and Bruno, who are all promising young cricketers.

This Ross ladies team photo includes a young Sarah Potter who also played for the West of England with Colleen Rogers and Jo Greaves of Woolhope Cricket Club. Sarah went on to play for the England ladies in the same team as Rachel Heyhoe Flint. Sarah played in seven test matches and six one-day internationals and scored one test century. She is the daughter of the late Dennis Potter, the author, who lived in Ross. Sarah was also a good hockey player, representing Herefordshire for whom she was a prolific goal scorer. The photograph shows Colleen Rogers front left, Pam Evans (Captain) front middle and Sarah Potter with headband.

Canon Frome Ladies enjoy their share of the celebrations when photographed with a number of honours achieved in the 1970s.

Standing L to R: Pat Smith, Yvonne Evans, Sally Hunt, Angela Stock, Hazel Beavan, Tom Evans, Janet Pearce, ? Whitaker, Hati Thurtle, Georgina Mathews, Philip Powell, Andrew Whitaker, Charlie Davies, Vera Davies, Philip Hunt, Elliot Davies.
Sitting Front row L to R: Betty Hunt, Elsie Evans, Joan Powell, Gertie Goode, Susan Hunt, n/k, Sandra Whitaker.
The trophies won that season were Woolhope Six-a-Side, Fox at Bransford Six-a-Side, Brockhampton K/O Cup, and the Canon Frome Six-a-Side Cup.

Lady cricketers at Eastnor Circa 1900.

Eileen Sandford has spent more years than she cared to remember giving support to her husband and Eastnor Cricket Club veteran Jim Sandford. She is in the photograph serving teas with her colleague Maria Ferreira.

Burghill & Tillington Ladies fund raising, August 1974.

"I knew it! Letting 'em play cricket at Lord's was the thin end of the wedge."

Women's Cricket Association

March 2009 saw **Charlotte Edwards** captain England to a 5 wicket victory over New Zealand in the one day World Cup final at the Sidney Oval in Australia. This was followed up by them again beating New Zealand by 8 wickets in the ICC 20/20 World Cup final at Lords in June. Charlotte can be seen with Herefordshire's Marsha Davies in the Kent 2008 County Championship winning side below.

Kent Ladies Championship winning Team
Back row left to right: Penny Arnold, Alan Duncan (Coach), Emily Drumm (NZ), Hazel Lovegrove, Charlotte Edwards (Captain England), Laura Boorman, Natalie Lane (England under 19 captain), Emma Plush, Suzie Rowe, Malcolm Ings (Manager), Lynsey Askew (England).
Front row left to right: Lydia Greenway (England), Marsha Davies (England&Wales), Jo Watts (England), Laura Thompson.

Marsha Davies holding the County Championship Trophy outside Buckingham Palace (see over).

Marsha Davies was born in Pontypool on the 12th December 1978. She started her cricket career at Malvern Girls College in 1989 and is now a schoolteacher at Weobley School, and lives in Ross-on-Wye. She has captained Wales on five occasions and also played for England A against Australia and New Zealand.

In August 2005 Marsha and Ceri Griffiths, who was at Lady Hawkins school in Kington, were selected to play for Wales in the women's European championships at Cardiff. In 2006 and 2007 she was a member of the Kent ladies team that won the county championship. During 2006 Marsha went to South Africa and played indoor action cricket in a three cornered competition against South Africa and Australia, which, she said, was an eye opener. This set Wales in good shape for 2007 when they played in the ladies Indoor World Cup which was played at Bristol. This competition included South Africa, Australia, New Zealand, England and Wales, and it turned out to be successful for Wales because they won their first indoor match against the old enemy England. When Marsha retired from championship cricket she concentrated on coaching.

Harriet Lowe is the daughter of Tim Lowe who is the Chairman of the Hereford Cricket Society. Harriet was educated at the Cathedral School and in June 1999 played for the England Development cricket team. Shortly afterwards, she was selected as a reserve for the England Under-19 team, but unfortunately did not play. However, Harriet did play for the Worcestershire Ladies until joining the RAF, where she now plays. She also coaches the Combined Servises team.

Left: **Rachel Heyhoe Flint** has played in the county on numerous occasions and has been in the same team as some of Hereford born lady cricketers. She played for England between 1960 and 1979 in 22 Tests and 23 one-day internationals. Her crowning glory was captaining the winning world cup side in 1973, closely followed by being one of the first women to be admitted to the MCC. She also played international hockey and is now a successful journalist and broadcaster. Carol Roberts, wife of the late Jack, turned up to make up the numbers in a college match with Marsha Davies and ended up playing a side which included Rachel and was astounded to watch her stroke the ball around the ground magnificently.

Jo Greaves receiving the Player of the Year award at Woolhope Cricket Club in 2006. She also played for the West of England with Colleen Rogers and Sarah Potter.

Herefordshire can boast that the foundations of Ladies Cricket were laid in the County.

In 1926 **Molly Scott Bowden** formed the Ladies National Cricket Association in Colwall and since then this small village nestling in the shadow of the Malvern Hills has been a stronghold for Ladies Cricket, both at a local and National level. Many fine lady cricketers have played on the picturesque ground. There was a report in the Hereford Times in August 1929 confirming that Colwall hosted the 3rd ladies Cricket Festival thus confirming that it was well established by then. When Women's cricket recommenced after the war in 1945, sixty-six women cricketers assembled at Colwall to play three matches a day, and in 1951 two hundred players turned up for the Silver Jubilee of the Colwall Ladies Cricket week. More than half a century later Colwall is still a stronghold of ladies cricket. Rachel Heyhoe-Flint, the former England Captain, has taken part in the Colwall Festival alongside other England Players.

Above: The **English Ladies** team on a tour of Sri Lanka. **Colleen Rogers** of Woolhope Cricket Club and Ross Ladies is second from the left in the middle row.

CHAPTER V

Schools and Youth

Cricket in the county at school and youth level has always been competitive, and some of the photographs in this chapter show the depth of talent that Herefordshire has produced in the 20th century, and is still producing at the beginning of the 21st.

Many of these young cricketers attended Hereford Cathedral School, including Peter Richardson, who later played for Worcestershire and England, Matthew Parry, Keith Edwards, George and John Warley; also Eric Jenkins, John Chadd and Roger Pye. Local historian and author John Eisel is a scorer on the 1959 photograph. Between 1949 and 1954 the school employed Joe Woodward the former Nottinghamshire player as their grounds man. Schools and youth cricket is always the lifeblood for the future. The authors show in this Chapter that it has continued from the early part of the century up to the present day, and with the enormous amount of effort being put in by experienced local coaches they are sure it will continue strongly, long into the 21st century.

Many of the older cricketers in the county will remember starting to play cricket in the local meadows with oversized kit. Luckily today, facilities at grounds are very much better for young people learning to play the game.

Hereford Cathedral School 2nd XI in 1956
Back row left to right: J.C. Craig (Scorer), R.H. Vaughan, P.N. Boardman, Mr. J.W. Rowlands, H.J. Farrow, E.J.E. Evans.
Front row left to right: C.G. Marshall, A.N. Pritchard, P.F.W. Tozer, G.H. Dimmock (Captain), W.R. Pye, E.G. Toplis, P.T. James.
J.W. Rowlands became an RAF heavyweight boxing champion; C.G. Marshall was also captain of the school shooting team. E.G. Toplis was a reporter for the Hereford Times. Roger Pye, who kindly provided this photograph, played in local cricket all his life; he was at one time captain of Kington and he also played for Titley.

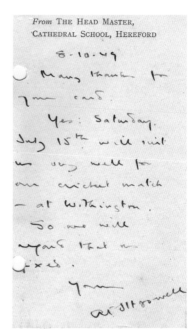

Hereford Cathedral School 1st XI Cricket in 1948. (Played 14 and won 14)
Back Row left to right: M. Gray, T.C.B. Porter, Mister R.D. Lancaster, D.J. Pill, J.P.L. Thomas.
Sitting left to right: G.T. Warley, B.A. Proctor, P.E. Richardson (Captain), P.K. Veale, H.C.W. Nicholls.
Front Row left to right: C.L. Davies, J.W. Warley, M. Allsebrook.
(Photo W.H. Bustin)

A Cathedral School fixture note to Withington Cricket Club dated 1949 from the Headmaster Mr. A.F.J. Hopewell, who coached many of the County's successful cricketers.

Hereford Cathedral School 1959
John Eisel, the scorer, is a well-known local historian and has written books on various aspects of Hereford History. Keith Edwards, a local builder, became a successful cricketer in Hereford
(Photo by Geoffrey Hammonds)

D. V. HART-DAVIES. I. R. MACLEOD. D. HUGHES. MR. J. L. T. BROOKS. R. CHATER. K. EDWARDS.
O. D. THOMAS. A. N. PRITCHARD. P. R. SHEPHERD (Capt.). P. A. LYNCH. I. A. D. FRENCH.
J. C. EISEL (scorer).
A. J. MEGGINSON

HEREFORD HIGH SCHOOL FOR BOYS.—1st CRICKET XI., 1923.

Hereford High School team in 1945

Hereford High School opened its doors in1912. The school produced one of Herefordshire's finest cricketers in **Reg Perks**, who went on to play for Worcestershire and England.

Back row from left to right: P. Johnson, L.P. Griffiths.
Middle row left to right: H. Collins, H.A. Farr, M. Pritchard, L. Lipwick.
Front row left to right: M.P. Robinson, P. Grubham, W.J. Bullock (Captain), J.T. Terry, M.B. Gage.

Lucton School 1952

Back Row, left to right: Fred Harwood (Scorer), David Turner, Cliff Davies, Geoff Pudge, Brian Leeke, Terry Anderson, Howard Meredith.
Front Row: David Small, Ernie Cole, Hugh (Taffy) Davies (Captain), Richard Evans, Richard Hall.

Lucton School 1st XI in 1958

Back row from left to right: K. Marshall (scorer); W.J. Jackson; ? Watson; ? Thomas, M. Abberley; M. Meredith, S. Edwards.
Front Row: G. Davies, D. Appleby, G. Farr, R.B. Williams, T. L. Williams.

Leominster Grammer School c.1950.

Back row: Ian Bruckner; n/k; Graham Mitchell, Richard Sparey, ? Strickland; n/k.
Front row: Len Beel; Geoff Beel; n/k; Rodney Grinnell; n/k; n/k.

An early photograph of **Leominster Grammar School** has been found recently. One of the team members is Chris Moyle (seated on the front row first left). Others (in no particular order) are Beavan, Pat Preece, Stanley Harvey, Arthur Wolstenholme, Reg Bishop and Tudor Thomas.

Tilley and Son, photo., Ledbury.

LEDBURY GRAMMAR SCHOOL CRICKET MATCH.
SONS V. FATHERS—THE OPPOSING TEAMS.

Ledbury Grammar School

The photographs were taken in the early part of the 20th century and show the tremendous enthusiasm that the town had for cricket at this time. The unique old pavilion is in the background with the team and supporters looking on.

1291. LEDBURY GRAMMAR SCHOOL MATCH. SONS V FATHERS.

First Ledbury Colts Team after the Second World War 1946

Back row left to right: J. Barnett, R. Newman, P. Pitt, M. Leach.

Front row, left to right: B. Messam, M. Paul, G. Yapp, S. Bramley, B. Basters, G. Symonds, I. Collet.

Ross Grammar School Junior Side in 1940
The teacher in the photograph is Mr Edward West and the team is as follows:-
Back row, left to right: Gordon Witts, Peter Pascoe, Geoff Williams, David Rudge, John Evans.
Front row left to right: Jim Roberts, Roger Hicks, Rex Roff (Captain), Martin Steward, Roy Pittaway.

(Rex Roff from Ross Cricket Club produced this old school photograph)

Roger Hicks became a reporter on the Ross Gazette.

Lady Hawkins School Cricket Team 1940
Back row: Eric Emmett; David Goodwin; Gerald Knowles; Edward Robinson; Robert Jenkins; Francis Price; Thomas Pugh.
Middle row: Alfred Smith; Anthony Price; Albert Gurmin; Sydney East; John Evans.
Front row: Peter Galvin; Brian Owens.

The **Ross Cricket Club, under 13** team in September 2007. They won the youth League and Cup.

Back row left to right: Harry King, Michael Jeffries, Peter Sykes (Secretary Hereford Cricket Board), Gabriel Warwick, David Peacock.

Centre row, left to right: Chris Mair, Bob Castles, Ed Cinderey.

Front Row left to right: David Long, Alex Davies, Dale Brooke, Joe Tumelty.

Herefordshire under 16 county squad in 2001
Back row, left to right: Edward Price (Coach), Tom Harper, Ian Massey, Stuart Jennings, Wayne Dade, Ewen Moore, Adam Hewlett, Ashley Nahorniak, Mark Hanschell (Manager).
Front row: Tom Brierley, Andrew Sherlock, Dale Withers, Stephen Caple, Andrew Price, Henry Langford, Oliver Williams.

Queen Elizabeth Grammar School Bromyard XI 1950

The team played on the Grammar School ground near the old railway sidings on the Tenbury Wells road and had an attractive pavilion. The Bromyard Grammar School Foundation, which is a charity, owns the ground. At present the ground is leased to the Bromyard Folk Festival Ltd who sub-let it to the current occupiers Bromyard Football Club for their junior team. Unfortunately the pavilion looks the worse for wear and is being considered for demolition.

Back row L to R: Dick Davies (scorer), Geoffrey Firkins, David Cave, Norman Cooper, Bill James, Tom Lainchbury, Raymond Jones.
Front row L to R: Dennis Hughes, Geoffrey James, Colin Robinson (capt), David Barnes, Pat Dallow, Rod Philpot (12th man).

Herefordshire County under 13 girls team.
A photograph of the successful side that beat Shropshire in 2006. Shropshire scored 137 runs for 4 wickets and Herefordshire reached their target with only 5 balls to spare.

Back row left to right: Ian Johnson (Manager), Kate Bishop, Gabby Williams, Rebecca Smith, Daisy Powles, Louisa Smith, Kate Trounson, Steve Large (Coach).
Front row left to right: Kate Farmer, Hannah Lines, Renee Johnson, Ella Johnson, Georgette Williams.

Wormelow Cricket club under 15 team
The team were very successful in 2007 winning the league and cup double.

Back row, left to right: Peter Blair, Marcus Ashcroft, Eddie Combes, Nigel Evans (Manager/Coach), Tom Cutler, Richard Pritchard, Ben Bradley.

Front row, left to right: Tom Craig, Chris Parry, Ashley Weston, Dan Hearn, Luke Jones.

Weobley Grammar School under 14 team in 1987.

The photograph shows the members of the victorious team who beat Belmont Abbey School to win the Chadd Cup. It was a close match and they won by one run off the last ball. The team represented Hereford the following season in the Lord Taverners Cricketers Colts competition.

Back row left to right: Jonathon Smith, Ben Bayliss, Ian Carpenter, Jonathon Cooke, Gareth Watkin, Richard Wood.
Front row left to right: Tristan Bartholomew, Paul Rymarz, Graham Smith, Duncan Verry (Captain), Andrew Jones, Mark Hurds.

Elms School under 12 winners of the Calypso Cup in 2001.

Back row left to right: George Stafford, Henry Cruickshank, Lonan O'Herlihy, Chris Fenton, Ben Hamilton, Monty Flint, Charles Weston.

Front row left to right: Ben Jones, Peter Bailey, Jamie McKee, Charles Frost, Alex Brierley.

Owen Davies from Golden Valley pictured in his School Days at Worcester King School in 1929. He is seated on the ground front left. He played for the Worcestershire Nursery Team in 1936.

Shobdon Youth

Bromyard under eleven's in 2006.
Back row left to right: -
Rhys Owens, Nick Dent, Lee Taylor,
Josh Weaver, Luke Hadley, Thomas
Bayliss.
Front row left to right:-
Daniel Masters, Ian Bullock, Nick
Leighton, John Parker, Alex Parker.

St Owens & Bluecoat 1928
Back Row: J. Sawyer, n/k, J.Jay, J. Morgan.
Middle Row: D. Preece, Mr. Morgan, J. Silvester, (Captain) Mr. Meyrick, A Everard.
Front Row: G. Almrott, S. Williams, R. Richards.

CHAPTER VI

Herefordshire County Cricket Club & City Clubs

In this chapter the authors have concentrated on the Herefordshire County Cricket Club and clubs located in Hereford City.

Herefordshire Minor Counties Cricket Club can boast some of the most picturesque grounds to host their matches in the Minor Counties League including:-

Luctonians cricket club ground is set in the village of Kingsland and whilst the ground is large and open, the club has superb changing, dining and socialising facilities and the club extends a friendly atmosphere to any visitors. Probably the most exciting match at Luctonians was when Herefordshire beat Middlesex in the NatWest Trophy.

Eastnor cricket ground is set in rolling countryside between Ledbury and Malvern. The club boasts a new modern pavilion to compliment their original 19th century pavilion, which still stands on site. Eastnor cricket ground is unique in Herefordshire as it is overlooked by Eastnor Castle

Kington cricket club is at the Recreation Ground, Mill Street, surrounded by old trees which gives it a very intimate feel. Kington has a first class pavilion and an ancient seating enclosure. The Club have hosted many Minor County games but the most prestigious match they hosted was Herefordshire v Yorkshire in the NatWest Trophy.

Colwall Cricket Club is set near the Malvern Hills in the village centre and was the home of the ladies National Cricket Association which was formed in the early part of the last century. The club supports two grounds and an old pavilion. Colwall have hosted many first class players benefit matches, and also Minor Counties games.

The HOLT CUP 1992
SHROPSHIRE v HEREFORDSHIRE
played at Shrewsbury
on Sunday 17th May 1992

SHROPSHIRE			HEREFORDSHIRE		
J.Foster	b.D.C.M.Robinson	56	H.V.Patel	c.Edmunds b.A.P.Pridgeon	89
J.B.R.Jones	b.S.D.Verry	61	G.J.Lord	c.Davidson b.B.K.Shantry	18
T.Parton	c.Watkins b.S.D.Verry	47	D.J.R.Martindale	c.Foster b.A.B.Byram	21
M.R.Davies	not out	37	S.G.Watkins	b.G.Edmunds	32
M.Davidson	not out	18	R.M.Cox	l.b.w. b.A.P.Pridgeon	13
G.L.Home			R.P.Skyrme	run out	11
A.B.Byram			M.F.D.Robinson	not out	17
A.P.Pridgeon			D.J.Mokler	c.Home b.A.S.Barnard	6
A.S.Barnard			S.D.Verry	not out	9
B.K.Shantry			G.Smith		
G.Edmunds			D.C.M.Robinson		
	extras	15		extras	19
	TOTAL	234		TOTAL	235

1-90, 2-173, 3-191,

M.F.D.Robinson	11 - 2 - 0 - 52
S.D.Verry	10 - 2 - 2 - 34
G.Smith	11 - 2 - 0 - 48
D.C.M.Robinson	11 - 4 - 1 - 24
S.G.Watkins	10 - 0 - 0 - 46
R.M.Cox	2 - 0 - 0 - 19

1-32, 2-76, 3-151, 4-185, 5-199, 6-211, 7-219,

A.P.Pridgeon	11 - 2 - 2 - 51
B.K.Shantry	11 - 1 - 1 - 39
A.S.Barnard	10 - 1 - 1 - 34
G.Edmunds	11 - 0 - 1 - 39
A.B.Byram	11 - 0 - 1 - 61

HEREFORDSHIRE WON BY THREE WICKETS
Herefordshire C.C.C's. first Cup-Limited Over match in a Minor Counties Competition

Umpires C.Smith, W.Morgan,   Scorers J.A.Jones, G.C.Wood

In May 1992 Herefordshire played their first limited over match in a Minor Counties Competition against Shropshire. The photograph is of the Scorecard of the match, which Herefordshire won by three wickets. The beautifully hand written scorecard was created by Gordon Wood and confirms that the art of calligraphy is not dead.

BROCKHAMPTON

CRICKET CLUB
FOUNDED 1897

A tranquil scene at Brockhampton in 1999 when Herefordshire defeated Wiltshire by 80 runs in their first ever home National Westminster cup match in the second round of the competition.

In 2006 three local cricketers scored half centuries in the same game for Herefordshire in the Minor Counties Championship against Devon at Torquay.
Left to right: Henry Langford from Brockhampton, David Exall from Kington and Ashley Nahorniak also from Brockhampton.

New 21st Century Brockhampton Club House.

Chris Burroughs and **Gwynne Jones**.
Chris is a fine batsman, bowler and captain of Herefordshire. The photo shows him flying the flag to celebrate the county's 2002 success (see below) and winning the Wilfred Rhodes Batting Trophy for topping the Minor Counties batting averages in the same year. Gwynne Jones is Chairman of the Herefordshire Minor Counties Cricket Club.

Herefordshire -v- Norfolk 2002.

The match manager in the photograph, Derek Hince, started playing cricket at Burley Gate with his brother Ray. He then joined Hereford City Sports Club and was a versatile wicket keeper batsman. When he finished playing he was appointed to Herefordshire Minor Counties Committee. He has served the county side with distinction both as match manager and advertising co-ordinator.

Photograph of Herefordshire County Cricket Club before their successful Minor Counties championship final against Norfolk at Luctonians in 2002.
The members on the photograph are: back row, left to right: Jim Morris (scorer), Rob Hughes, Karl Pearson, Nick Davies, Simon Roberts, Martin McCague (ex England), Paul Lazenbury, Duncan Willets, Harshad Patel, John Beaman (promotions). Front row left to right: Derek Hince (match manager), Aamir Farooque, Kevin Cooper, Gwynne Jones (chairman), Chris Burroughs, Bryan Smith (committee), Ismail Dawood, Peter Sykes (secretary).

AFTER LOSING TO WORCESTER AT SOCCER IN A REPRESENTATIVE GAME, HEREFORD TURNED THE TABLES ON THEIR TRADITIONAL RIVALS AT CRICKET WHEN THE CITY EVENING LEAGUE XI BEAT THEIR NEIGHBOURING COUNTERPARTS BY 20 RUNS.

Sketched are some of the Hereford players who played a major part in the victory —

STAN MARSTON retired hurt after scoring 17

KEITH EDWARDS who took 4 for 26

A sharp FROST (Dave) in the field

and IAN MACKLIN who hit a splended 57 not out

In 1964 Hereford artist Peter Manders paid a visit to Widemarsh Common where he sketched some of the Hinton Youth Club players on their meeting with Herefordians B in the Evening League knock out cup competition.

The cartoon was featured in Peter's Saturday Sketchbook newspaper column.

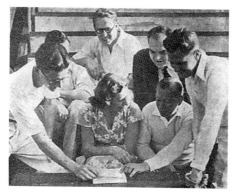

An Accountants XI organized by accountant Peter Hill played the Inland Revenue in 1952. It is no surprise that the two teams are checking the final totals very carefully!

Gerald, Ivan and Stephen, the Bishop cricketing family.

Ivan was well known in Hereford cricketing circles, he was Secretary of the Hereford Evening League and a member of the umpires association.

Stephen played for Shop Assistants 2nds from his early teens and he was also in the Herefordshire Schoolboys squad. Gerald was Captain of Anvil Enterprises Evening League side until the company folded. Anvil then reformed as Widemarsh.

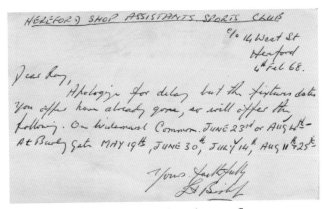

This was typical of the correspondence between fixture Secretaries who were trying to fix a busy fixture list when local cricket was in its hey day.

Anvil Enterprises CC was formed by Tony Body and captained by Gerald Bishop, son of Ivan Bishop who was secretary of the Hereford Evening League. They played their home matches initially on the King George VI playing fields in Hereford. The club originated from the odd friendly match between the works and staff members, and Anvil played at Bromyard from about 1973.

In 1976 Anvil had progressed to Division 2 of the Hereford Evening League when Peter Manders was let loose with his pencils on 12th June and produced another notch for his Saturday sketchbook in the Hereford Times. The club then amalgamated with Westfields and played under the name of Widemarsh when Phil Hallett and Dennis James (son of Les) joined the side.

Reproduced by kind permission of Peter Manders; Sat June 12th 1976.

Saunders Valves 1964 Dinner Dance

Back row left to right: Nat Cartwright, Mick Carroll, Nigel Yarwood, Simon Swancott, Ollie Tooze, Arthur Ridler.
Front row left to right: Mick Williams, Tony Body, Bill Morris, John Dewey, and Bob Downes. (Photo by Nigel Yarwood)

B.T.H. 1960

Back row left to right: Harry Miles (Umpire), Roy Hide, Terry Davies, Nigel Yarwood, and Frank ?, n/k, Elton Morgan, John Powell (umpire)
Front row left to right: Vince Preece, Cyril Legg, Dick Chawner, Arthur Crabtree, John Hall, Alan Jones.

Harcourts, who later became A.E.I at Rotherwas. This headed notepaper confirms the support given to their own social and sports teams by local industry. They became AEI from about 1957 until 1964, then Smart & Brown 1965 until 1969 and finally Thorn Lighting, until the closure of the factory.

HARCOURTS SOCIAL & ATHLETIC CLUB

ROTHERWAS, HEREFORD

PRESIDENT:
N. DENNES, ESQ.

CHAIRMAN:
H. E. BROOKS, ESQ.

TELE. 3035·6

SECRETARY:
MR. E. PREECE

TREASURER:
MR. E. J. MOON

The original team to play on the Rotherwas ground was the Rotherwas side. There was a rumour that during the 2nd World War an old railway engine was buried on the ground. The pavilion was built in about 1955 and was used until the ground ceased to be a sports ground.

The team were playing in the Evening League in 1952 when they came second in Division Two. The club used the ground until about 1971 when Hereford United Football Club used it for training for about three years. Westfields Football Club became tenants in 1974 until they moved to their new ground at Widemarsh in about 2004.

Under the name of AEI they were Division Two winners in 1960 and runners up in 1958, and in that year they had a dinner dance the photo at the dance includes Nigel Yarwood who played cricket in Herefordshire for many years and is referred to in Ch 11. Under Ediswan they were runners up in Div 2 in 1950 and 1953. The photograph shows the team in that era. They won Div 3 as Smart & Brown in 1968 and 1971. The ground has now been sold for development within the industrial estate.

Painter Bros Cricket Team were formed after the 2nd World War to play in the Hereford Evening League. Painter Bros 1963.

Back Row left to right: John Sellers, Syd Catley, Les Campbell, Bill Fairclough, Clive Trenchard, George Hyde. Front Row: Roger Smith, Tony Meredith, Colin Morris, John Bradley, John Bevan.

NALGO won the Coronation Cup in its inaugural year 1953. The cup was presented by Colonel Thornycroft to commemorate the coronation of Queen Elizabeth II. The competition carried on for many years in the form of a six players a side competition of five overs with each outfield player bowling an over of six balls. The venue was the racecourse and the competition was run by Hereford City Sports Club.

NALGO 1950 Team:
Back Row left to right: B. Rutherford, E. Monkhouse, J. Terry, E. Pitt, R. Roberts, B. Cutler, J. Donaldson (scorer). Front row left to right: Ted Johnson, John Smallbone, R. Williams, Bryan Smith, Neville Sandford.

Saracen's Head 1987 Junior Cup Winners.

Back Row left to right: Frank Edwards, Les Powell, Steve Keen, Eric Pritchard, Chris Gallagher, Roger Eames, Keith Brisland.
Front Row: Clive Eames, Steve Deem, John Marston, Dave Brookes, Chris Lea, Brian Preece.

Wyevale Division 3 Evening League winners 1983.

Standing: Jean & Terry Preece, Bert Williams, Jack Maine, George Warley, Alwyn Buchanan, n/k.
Sitting: Gerry Gilbert, John Causer, Ron Taylor, Eddie Taylor, n/k.

In the mid 1950s Wyevale won the Hereford City Sports Club six-a-side tournament beating A.E.I. by 5 runs off the last of the match. Eric Jenkins and Les James were the dominant batsmen for Wyevale.

Wayfarers Cricket Club was formed in 1962 by a consortium of Schoolteachers headed by Alan May and Glyn Jones who were both teachers at Redhill School at the time.

Wayfarers 1962
Back row: n/k, Jerry?, Ian Pond, Brian Thomas, Gordon Hiley, Tony Bailey.
Front row: n/k, Alan May, Glyn Jones, n/k, Hugh Ward.
Other members who played regularly during the 1960s were Derek Jones, Stewart Blyth, Brian Tipping, Ken Hook, Keith Williams and Dave Marchant.

THE
**WAYFARERS
CRICKET CLUB**

FIXTURES 1962

Wyesiders was formed by Jack Roberts and Alan Taylor in 1977. The team was made up mostly from teachers and pupils from the 6th Form College and Aylestone School. The home ground for the team was at Aylestone School. The Hereford Doctors team eventually became part of Wyesiders.
Back row: Richard Bridges, Andy Legge, n/k, Craig Patton, David Bird, n/k.
Front row: David Jennings, Peter Richards, Bruce Freeman, Jack Roberts, Andrew Bridges.

MEB were formed in 1953 to play in the Hereford Evening League. They were a very successful team for decades until they ceased playing in the 1980s.

M.E.B. in action

The batsman will now never be allowed to forget this day when Bert Smart gave him out in an MEB Evening League game in the 1950s. The sprightly looking fielder in the top left hand corner is Ernie Ridger who was captain of the Thynnes works team in the Evening League. The cat-like figure behind the stumps is Ray Hill who played local cricket for many years. Brian Smart supplied this superb action photograph.

M.E.B. circa 1955
Standing left to right: W.G. Ellson (Manager), Harry Marks, Len Beavan, Rolf (Ernie) Francombe, Brian Messam, Maurice Murdock, Graham Doody, Neville Corner, Ted Pearman (umpire).

Sitting: Robin Buchanan, Wilf Palfrey, Gordon Lamputt, Alan Edwards, Stan Marston.

Bulmers 1935

This team photo of a pre-war Bulmers team includes a few well-known local cricketers including Reg Michael who played a major role at Pontrilas and Ewyas Harold Cricket Clubs, and Lloydy George, who was the Landlord of the Horse & Groom Public House in Hereford for many years and in his younger days played football for Hereford United where he also became a Director. Two other players in the team, A. Oliver and A. Wardell, also played football for Hereford United in the 1930s.

Back Row left to right: G. Butterworth, A. Oliver, M. Hills, J. Butterworth, C. Blackwell, H. Rogers, P. Adams, R. Michael, W. Clinkett, L. Davies, W. Shinn.
Front Row left to right: S. Heir, B. Watkins, L. George, A. Wardell, E.F. Bulmer, S. Lampitt, G. Wood, B. Hicks, T. Howls.

Bulmers circa 1960
Left to right: Rodney Lodge, Don Bateman, Les James, (hidden Dennis Barlow), Geoff Wood, Clive Gibbons, n/k, Roy Wood, and Russell Davies.

The ticket for Bulmer's annual dinner dance 1963 confirms how things have changed over the years. The venue was a pub, which no longer exists, and the price was the grand sum of 29 Shillings per couple, which is equal to 75p each in 2009.

Alf Marston with son Stan playing for Bulmers in May 1964.

Wiggin Cricket Club in 1984

Back row: Selwyn Williams, George Bull, Cedric Davies, Derek Allison, Geordie Harbottle,
Dave Hudson, unknown young lady.
Front row left to right: Robin Griffiths, n/k, Peter Sykes (Captain), Bill Nicholls, Alec Carter.
Inset: (top) Richie Thwaites and Fraser Cornish.
The photo shows a successful side in the 1984 season. Cedric Davies scored his maiden and only half century.

The photograph is of a very casual **Hinton Cricket Club** Team in 1946. Second on the top left is Jim Finney who became a first class football referee.

Back, left to right: n/k, Jim Finney, Jim Wiltshire, Harry Inight. Front Left to right: 4th Les (Keki) Davies (remainder unknown)

In 1964 Hereford artist Peter Manders paid a visit to Widemarsh Common where he sketched some of the **Hinton Youth Club** players on their meeting with Herefordians B in the Evening League knock out cup competition.

Left to right: Glyn Rees, Jack Richards, Mick Harman, Charlie Phipps, and Colin Jennings. They were featured in his Saturday Sketchbook newspaper column.

Hereford United FC Cricket Team

On Sunday 30th June 1959 at Much Marcle, **Hereford United Football Club** formed a team to take on **Westons Sports CC**. The game was organised by Len Weston of Westons Cider Company who was at the time chairman of Hereford United. The team was as follows:

Back row left to right: Gerald Evans, Mel Rooke, Gerry Sewell, Mr. Len Weston, Jimmy Lee, Roly Morris, Keith Edwards. Front row left to right: Joe Wade (ex Arsenal,) then the manager of Hereford United, Dick Richardson (Worcestershire & England) with Robert Wade, Henry Horton (Hampshire), Roy Williams and Graham Perkins.

Keith Edwards is a local man who was educated at the Cathedral School, where he started his cricketing career. However his early claim to fame came as a footballer. He joined Hereford United in 1959 after serving an apprenticeship with Birmingham City. He spent three years with Hereford United before moving on to Gloucester City. When he left school he spent three years at Hereford City Sports Club but in 1959 he was informed by Len Weston the chairman of Hereford United that he was now playing for Weston Sports.

Keith dutifully accepted the terms, and rejoined Hereford City Sports Club, when he moved to Gloucester City in 1963 to play football, and had many successful seasons as a bowler in a team that included John Chadd, Bryan Smith, Norman Davies, Peter Harrison and Neville Symonds. In 1969 Keith had his most successful season, taking 120 wickets in the weekend league and 60 in the evening league. One of his most memorable games was against Lydney at the racecourse when he took his only 10-wicket haul. He had got the first 9 wickets under his belt when John Chadd came on to bowl at the other end. John apparently bowled a beautifully flighted ball with plenty of air, the batsman went up the wicket to slot it over mid off when the inevitable happened: the batsman got a thick outside edge and the ball flew like a bullet to gully where Keith was fielding. He swiftly took a very impressive catch off his captains bowling! Later that season he went on to take 5 wickets in 5 balls against Plymouth. Shortly afterwards Keith was honoured with the Three Counties League player of the season award.

The Hereford Doctors XI was formed 1976. The first captain was Jeff Kramer, who it is rumoured would set his field by walking to the wicket look around and say 'right spread out'! Some other captains of the side were John Wood, Ian Ferguson, Julian Wheeler, H. Connor, Bob Izon, C. Frith and Peter Wilson. The team eventually amalgamated with Wyesiders CC.

Dr Julian Wheeler recalled playing a match against the local vicars, when their opening bowler delivered a lovely swinging ball to one of the men of the cloth who got a definite outside edge, which all the close fielders heard. Dr John Wood was acting wicketkeeper on the day and much to his surprise the ball lodged securely in his gloves. With that a huge appeal was made, but the curate umpiring showed no interest and gave not out! The batsman, looking embarrassed, stood his ground, which left the fielding side in shock! The wicketkeeper turned to the vicar batting, looked into his eyes and said "and you a man of God!" With that the vicar turned and walked! (See picture overleaf).

Hereford Doctors' XI
Back row: Adrian Thomas, David Malins, Mike Allen, Tim Coleman, John Wood, Ian Reynolds, Peter Johnstone (Lord Taverners. Hon. Doctor for the day)
Front row: Peter Richards, Steve Watkins, Henry Connor, Peter Wilson, Julian Wheeler, Andrew Corfield.

A modern-day **Herefordshire Gents** team playing the Warwickshire Imps at Edgbaston.
Back row: L-R Warwickshire Umpire; Nick Osbourne; n/k; Richard Flynn; n/k; Roy Wargen; Nick Nenadich; Umpire Tony Capon.
Front row: Alan Meredith; Richie Price; Dave Mockler; Andrew Sockett; Rob Watkins.

The photograph below shows the **Hereford National Westminster Bank** team that won the West Midlands and Wales regional inter departmental cup final in 1977.

Some of the members of the team played for other teams in Herefordshire, namely Paul Simmons for Lads Club, Ted Partington for Herefordians and Richard Head who lived at Much Dewchurch and played at Wormelow.

Back row L to R: Alan Johnston, n/k , Geoff Myers, Martin Powell, Kevin Dye, Keith Brimble.
Front row L to R: R Simmons, H.A.D Salter, Richard Head, Roger Marsden, Ted Partington.

Gas Board Dinner 1950, celebrating winning the Leominster Senior and Junior Cups.
Standing: Ray G. Jones, Reg Griffiths, Ray Jones, John Godfrey, Tommy Hobson, Denis Barlow, Cyril Williams, Barry Hill, George Shutt, Ken Williams.
Sitting: Mr. Hobson (manager) Bill Griffiths, Don Preece, Bill Jones, (Capt) Geoff Wood, Bernard Shaw.

They played on the same ground as Painters behind Denco in Holmer Road Hereford underneath a large gasometer, perhaps Hereford's answer to the Oval! The team were formed in 1946 and played until 1965. and they were Division One winners in 1948 and 1950 and Division Two winners in 1958. Gas Board completed a unique double in the 1950s when they won the Leominster Junior Cup, were invited to compete in the Senior Cup and promptly won that as well, beating Bromyard in the final. They were reformed in the 1980s to play in the Evening League and they continued playing until the League folded in 2002.

**B.R.S.A.
six-a-side winners.**
This is a B.R.S.A. side who won the company six-a-side competition in 1968. Middle in the front is Molly Jones wife of Trevor who not only scored for B.R.S.A. but helped with the teas. She also scored for both Burghill St Mary's and Garnons for many years.

Back row L to R: Trevor Jones, Bob Hughes, Colin Wooley, Ernie Lloyd.

Front row L to R: Brian Jones, Molly Jones (scorer), Laurie Steele.

St. Mary's Burghill 1985

Back row (L to R): Mick Carroll, Trevor Jones, Julian Wheeler, Graham Rooke, Alan Jones, Ian Strangward , Tim Coleman

Front Row: Val Treagus, Ian Ferguson, Terry Matthews, John Wade.

CHAPTER VII

County Towns

19th Century photograph of an early Hereford Cricket Team.

The photograph was owned by Charles Evans and given by him to Hereford Reference Library. Copied for this book by kind permission of Robin Hill, Hereford Reference Library.

Hereford Cricket Club in 1910

Hereford Cricket Club in 1939. Match played on Sunday August 27 1939 between a Worcestershire XI and Mr. C.E.N. Shorting's 15 of Hereford & District for the benefit of C.H. Bull's testimonial fund. The sum realised was £51-15s-1d. This game was the last one played before the outbreak of the Second World War.
Team back row left to right: E.E. Gallimore, J.C. Smith, H.R. Hunt-Hicken, C.E.N. Shorting, J. Wood, D. Wargent, S.R. Cooper, D. Rabjohn, F. Davis, D. West. R.W. Roff, G. Thornycroft, W. Lawrence, S. Bullar, W.K. Plant, Lieutenant Col. C.M. Thornycroft, R. Jenkins, A. P. Singleton, G. Morris, W. Harris, J. Goodwin, J.V. Grindon, P.F. Jackson.
Front row left to right: B.P. King, R. Howarth, Hon. C.J. Lyttelton, Dr. Woodpower, R.T.D. Perks, E.Cooper, S. Martin, H.Yarnold.

Hereford City Sports Club Ist XI and reigning champions of The Beach Villas Three Counties League in the 1980s.

Back row left to right: Ernie Morgan, Rob Watkins, Phil Hunt, Andy Chadd, Tracy Goodwin, Dave Griffiths, Keith Edwards, Robbie Powell.

Front row: Andy Sockett, Ken Watson (Captain), Richard Skyrme.

Cricket seems to be a magnet for characters both on and off the field of play with many stories to be told. One such relates to a match played between the Sports Club and **Usk** in the mid 1960s. Usk had a very aggressive fast bowler and members of the club did not always appreciate his actions. One of his worst habits was when a batsman played the ball back to him. He would gather the ball in quickly and if he thought that the batsman was slightly out of his crease he threw the ball in the general direction of the batsman and the stumps in a mischievous manner not caring which one he hit!!

Ernie Morgan, to whom it happened on more than one occasion, recalled one particular incident. John Chadd was batting in his normal position, namely towards the tail end of the innings, and played a perfectly normal and good forward defensive stroke. The ball rolled back to the bowler. John anticipated the bowler's reaction and stood outside his crease. As the ball came whizzing towards him he turned inside and pulled it to mid wicket over the boundary with feeling, giving the bowler a fleeting glance at the same time. A lone sarcastic Welsh voice boomed out from the boundary: "serves ewe right ewe cocky b*****d!"

Hereford 1st XI in 1973

Back row left to right: Roy Humphries (scorer), Neville Symonds, Alan Jones, Mick Hayward, Clive Brazier, Tom Langford, Graham Smith, Norman Davies, Harry Miles (umpire).

Front row left to right: Keith Edwards, John Chadd, Mike Rose, Ernie Morgan.

In the back row 6th from the left is Tom Langford who was groundsman at Hereford for many years and prepared a number of superb pitches for Worcestershire County Cricket Club first class matches held at the Racecourse ground. Shortly afterwards Worcestershire offered tom the post of grounds man at New Road where he stayed until he retired from full time work.

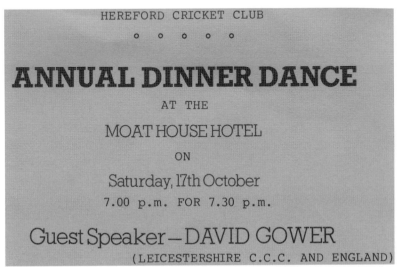

HEREFORD CRICKET CLUB

o   o   o   o   o

ANNUAL DINNER DANCE

AT THE

MOAT HOUSE HOTEL

ON

Saturday, 17th October

7.00 p.m. FOR 7.30 p.m.

Guest Speaker – DAVID GOWER

(LEICESTERSHIRE C.C.C. AND ENGLAND)

Hereford Cricket Club Dinner Dance Ticket.
David Gower was the former England Captain.

Hereford City Sports Club
(Cricket Section)

COL. THORNEYCROFT TROPHY

SIX-A-SIDE
TOURNAMENT

18th July, 1965 on the Racecourse

at 12-0 p.m.

Official Programme - 6d.

OFFICIALS

President : R. E. H. BAILY Esq., C.B.E.

Captain : Mr. J. E. CHADD

Tournament Marshal : Mr. N. E. PRITCHARD

Stewards :

Messrs. E. H. T. RIDGER, L. D. CARTER, M. PRITCHARD,

Umpires :

By courtesy of the Hereford Evening Amateur Cricket League Umpires Association.

(Members of Midland Counties Cricket Umpires Association)

The Hereford City Sports C'ub is indebted for the assistance and co-operation of Mr. Reg Williams, Hon. Sec of the Hereford Amateur Evening Cricket League and the Hereford Evening Amateur Cricket League Umpires Association.

This Programme entitles the holder to a FREE ticket in a ballot for a £3 Premium Bond and a £2 Premium Bond.

976

Hereford City Sports Club six a side programme in 1965.

HEREFORD CITY SPORTS CLUB
(Cricket Section)

SIX-A-SIDE
TOURNAMENT

21st JULY, 1968 at 11.30 A.M.

on

RACECOURSE GROUND, GRANDSTAND ROAD, HEREFORD

Hereford City Sports Club v. Nalgo. 1967 Final

OFFICIAL PROGRAMME
AND PRIZE SCHEME

Nº 1199   1/-

PRIZES - 1. £3 Premium Bond. 2. £2 Premium

4. Prize Value 15/-. 5. Prize Va

Registered under the Betting, Gaming and L

Promoter : E. B. SMITH, 5, Sollars Close, W

HCSC 1968 Programme and Fixture Card

THE
HEREFORD CITY
SPORTS CLUB

Season 1968

Headquarters and Ground :
THE RACECOURSE, HEREFORD.
Telephone 3098

Madley Bumpkins: *Tracey Goodwin, Bob Gardiner, Martin Peak, Mike Rose, Neville Symonds, Dennis Fothergill.*

Kington

Kington Cricket Club was formed in 1844 and play on the very picturesque recreation ground in the town. They are the only Hereford club to win the National Village Cricket Knockout Cup, which they won in 1993 at Lords cricket ground, the home of English Cricket.

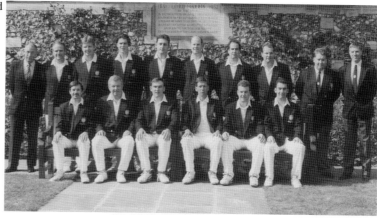

Right: **Kington Cricket Club at Lords**
Back row: David Hill (President), Mike Cronin, Dave Morgan, Rob Goodman, Rob Johnston, Clive Scott, Nigel Scott, Jim Lewis, David Phillips (Scorer), Carl Yeomans (Secretary). Front row: Kevin Gwynne, Rodney Bowdler, Alan Stansbury Stokes, Edward Price (Captain), Martin Powell, Mark Porteous.

Left: Basil D'Oliviera, the former England and Worcestershire all rounder, took a side to Kington in 1974-75 for his benefit year, and when he rang up to confirm the game he introduced himself to the lady who answered the phone and said "hello I am Basil D'Oliviera". She replied "yes and I am the Queen of England" and put the phone down.

Kington in 1960
Back row left to right: John Prater, Rob Andrews, David Appelby, Nigel Griffiths, Ted Nicholls, J. Prieby,
Front row left to right: Rodney Bowdler, Peter Smith, Roger Pye, (Captain), Tony Collins, (Captain in 1961), George Phillips.

Kington Cricket Club were the winners of the Leominster Knockout Cup at the Grange in the early 1960s

Back row left to right: Percy Briggs in hat, Percy was Robbie Richardson's father in law, and it was he who donated the Kington Knockout Cup to the club. Nick Faithful, Colin Campbell, John Evans, Rod Bowdler, Gerald Collett. Middle row left to right: George Phillips, Ian Scott, John Burgoyne.

Front row left to right: Brian Watts, Billy Nicholls, Robbie Richardson (captain), Mike Cronin, Peter Burgoyne. (Photograph courtesy of Allan Edwards)

In the early 1980s local businessmen in Kington came up with the idea of a competition for a Kington Trades six-a-side cricket trophy. The rules were quite simple:

(1) Each innings would consist of 5 overs.
(2) Each player would bowl one over per innings.
(3) Each team could have one guest cricketer.
(4) The other 5 players would be employees.

The matches were played at the Recreation Ground and Lady Hawkins School Ground by permission of Robbie Richardson. Many of the local residents turned out to watch this exciting competition.

Back row left to right: Michael East, David Belcher, Kerry Sergeant, Steve Evans.
Front row: Craig Brown (Australian), Allan Edwards, Nigel Evans, Darren Burns, Keith Jones, Andrew Weaver, David Simcock.

Kington Building Supplies played in the competition for many years under the strict(!) supervision of Allan Edwards, the Managing Director. Allan is the son of the late Bill Edwards who captained Kington Cricket Club in the 1950s. They won the competition on just one occasion. The photo shows the team in 1997/8, when the full side played a pre-tournament friendly match.

Ross-on-Wye

Ross 1925

1st team pictured outside the Hereford Cricket Club Pavilion before a league game on the 6th June 1925.
Back row: Maxstead, Thomas, Lane, Peachey, Taylor, Wilden. Front row: Ellis, R.W.P. Roff, Meredith, Abbot, West.
West on this photo is Stan West who is the brother of Don West; they were both regular first team players.

Grounds man Reg Preece & J. Woodward of the Falcons marking out Ross Cricket Ground 1932.

Ross -v- Falcons Touring Cricket Club 1932, walking to the old tea room on the bank with the old 19th century pavilion in the background.

Ross Cricket Club 1st XI in 1937

Back row Left to right: C. Downes, ? Kewley, Don West, Charles Peachey, Marmite Constance.
Front row left to right: R. Webb, n/k, R.W.P. Roff, n/k, J. Newton.

Don West is still alive aged 92. Don West's uncle, Stan (previous page), played for Ross in 1925.

Ross Cricket Club Saturday XI in 1957
Back row, left to right: R.G. Hicks, R.H.W.P. Roff, A. P. Notley, J. Sainsbury, L.J. Wall, E.J. Sainsbury, R.V. Bulgin.
Front row, left to right: D. West, R.W.P. Roff, K.A. Higton (captain), D.T. Ruck, H. Rushton, J. Pascoe.

Reginald W.P. Roff was the father of Rex Roff. He was born in Marlborough (Wiltshire) and moved to Ross in 1922, where he was an important part of Ross Cricket Club for many years. During his career with Ross he also played for Herefordshire, Monmouthshire and Gloucestershire. Ken Higton was captain of Ross scoring 1420 runs in 1929, which was then a club record. Don West now resides in Midhurst, West Sussex. He was a most successful batsman for the club, scoring 1000 runs for the First XI in 1946, 1947 and 1948. In addition he scored 1,000 runs in the matches he played in 1938 when he was only 20 years of age. Paul Notley beat Roff's 1949 club record in 1962 when he scored 1,047 runs in 34 innings with an average of 34.9.

The Ross New Pavilion was completed in 1965 at a cost of £22,000 to replace the 19th century pavilion shown on the Ross Gents photo in Ch 1 and below.

Reginald W.P. Roff scored 153 not out for Ross v Hereford on June 1927.

Ross Old Pavilion built in 1837 and recently refurbished.

ROSS-ON-WYE

CRICKET CLUB

SINGLE WICKET

Competition

for the

REX ROFF TROPHY

AT THE PARK, ROSS-ON-WYE

Commencing at 10.30 a.m.

SUNDAY, 28th AUGUST, 1966

Ledbury

Ledbury motif on 150th Anniversary tie.

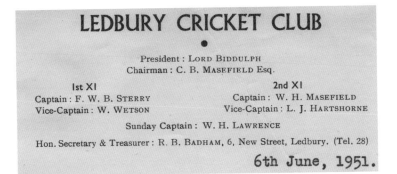

LEDBURY CRICKET CLUB

●

President : LORD BIDDULPH
Chairman : C. B. MASEFIELD Esq.

1st XI	2nd XI
Captain : F. W. B. STERRY	Captain : W. H. MASEFIELD
Vice-Captain : W. WETSON	Vice-Captain : L. J. HARTSHORNE

Sunday Captain : W. H. LAWRENCE

Hon. Secretary & Treasurer : R. B. BADHAM, 6, New Street, Ledbury. (Tel. 28)

6th June, 1951.

Ledbury Cricket Club letterhead, 1951.

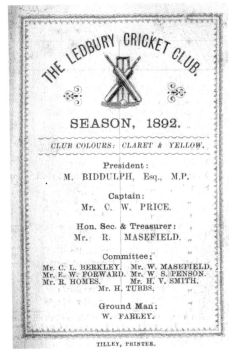

R & W Masefield shown on the 1892 fixture list.

Photo of an early time in Ledbury in 1890. The team was Ledbury Excelsiors. **Ledbury Cricket Club** is one of the oldest clubs in the county; they play on the ground behind the Full Pitcher Inn just outside the town centre. The team was at its peak in the 1940s and 50s when it was on a par with Hereford and was known to beat the city side.

Ledbury Presidents XI in July 1986
Back row: 1st left John Edwards; 1st right Phil Barnett.

Front row: 2nd left Jeff Fletcher; 3rd Grenville Box; 4th Bill Masefield (seated in tie); far right, 'Bumble Bates'

Steve Emery, who was born in Ledbury, played football for Hereford United and progressed to play in the Football League. He was a fine cricketer who played for Ledbury for many years during this period.

Ledbury in 1952

The team included some important names in Ledbury cricket in the post war years, namely Brian Messam, Bill Masefield, Brian Farley, Wilf Lawrence, and James Smith.
Back row left to right: P. Barnett, M. Thomas, R. Thurston, R. Badham, G. Ward, J. Chester, G. Richie, B. Messam, J. Suddes, N. Egerton, G. Jones.
Middle row left to right: R. Hale, G. Bryan, W. Masefield, W. Juckes, W. Lawrence, R. Lawrence, T. Watkins, I. Hunt, J. Smith, B. Farley.
Front row left to right: G. Wilkins, C. Williams, R. Jones, M. Evans.

The name Masefield is very much a part of Ledbury history and the family have been associated with the cricket club for over a century. George, a young solicitor, opened his practice in Ledbury in 1830 and started the family association with the club. His two sons, William and George Edward, played for the club. George Edward's son John became poet laureate. Bill Masefield, who was John's nephew, joined the club in 1946 after his demob from the Navy. Bill was stationed in Ceylon (Sri Lanka) and he played cricket there on coconut matting.

Bill took over the position of Fixture Secretary of Ledbury in 1947. He was Second XI Captain for 25 years, during the time that C.B. Masefield was chairman of the club. When C.B. Masefield died, Bill took over as chairman and later became President, thus maintaining the family's long association with the club.

Above: Wilf Lawrence, Captain of Ledbury and one of the County's great cricketers of the era. He hit 26 centuries and took over 1000 wickets.

The Wetson family Bill, John, Jack and Ernie, totalled 100 years service to the club. Ernie was most probably the best cricketer in the family; he was a fine opening bowler. The Juckes family, namely Fred in the late 19th century then his son Wally and finally David, have also given great service to the club. David played in the 1960s in the same team as Brian Messam, Frank Load, Jim Lee, Fred Sterry and Bob Badham.

Brian Messam's career with the club commenced in the mid 1950s following in the footsteps of Wilf Lawrence. Prior to Brian's arrival the most successful bowler was Wilf Lawrence, but with figures like 6 wickets for 14 runs against Hereford in the late 1950s Brian soon took over as the club's most successful bowler and he topped the bowling averages on a regular basis well into the 1960s.

James Smith, another fine cricketer who played for Ledbury, went on to represent Worcestershire sixteen times in the 1920s. He was a left hand batsman and a useful slow bowler. He was presented with the match ball mounted on a base when he took 10 wickets for 27 runs against Worcestershire Cinderella on August 13th 1932 when playing for Ledbury.

Leominster, winners of the Ludlow Six-a-Side

The town put together a good side and were not surprised that they won this competition. Many of the players went on to play for a number of years, and some are still playing the odd game.
Left to right: Jeremy Finney, Rob Thomas, Guy Morgan, Billy Harris, Mike Built, Jake Morgan.

Leominster in 1949 winning the Ludlow K/O Cup
Back row L-R: Alec Haines, Dennis Parker, Tom Howard, Dennis Arrowsmith, Billy Hall, N/K, Jim Merritts, Gordon Powell, and George Beale.
Front row L-R: Dai Davies, Jack Williams, Jack Beamand, Dick Burke, Bill Thomas.

Leominster

Leominster Cricket Club at Leominster Sports Club

Leominster fixture card in 1897. Leominster first played at the Grange in 1837. Note members' annual subscription: one old penny!

Back row left to right: Don Cahill, Dave Hodges, Richard Sparey, Steve Hodges, Jeremy Finney, Dave Barrington, Richard Marsh, Mark Morris, Dennis Parker.

Front row left to right: Anthony King, Russell Palmer, Richard Finney, Noel Withers, Adrian Gore.

150th Anniversary photograph 1987

Back row left to right: Tim Whitbread, Tim Sparey, Bill Meat, Alan Bowkley, Duncan Platford, Bill Kent, Paul Creshel, Dave Livesey, Nick Morris, Don Cahill, Brian Faulkner, Phil Barker, Andy Phillips, Richard Powell, Richard Marsh, James Sparey, Steve Grange, Richard Finney, Len Grange.

Front row (seated) left to right: Dorothy Platford, Noel Withers, Richard Sparey, Danny Morgan, Dennis Parker, Jeremy Finney, David Hodges, David Barrington, Adrian Gore, John Leddington Hill.

Bromyard

Because of its close geographical proximity to Warwickshire and Worcestershire many of both counties' first class players took advantage of Bromyard's facilities and generosity and played benefit matches at Bromyard. The Bromyard club was re-formed in 1953 and in the following years some of the first class players who took part included Dennis Amiss, who is named on the caption, and also Alvin Kallicharran, Vanburn Holder, Ron Headley, Mike Proctor, Sadiq Mohammad, Glenn Turner, Dipak Patel, Len Coldwell, Norman Gifford, Andy Lloyd, Chris Broad and Don Kenyon.

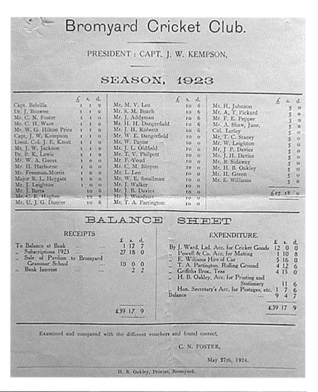

Bromyard and Stoke Prior are in this photograph, which was taken at the Grange Cricket Ground in Leominster in 1949. The competition was most probably the Leominster Knockout Cup. Regrettably not many of the players are known, those recognised are in the back row 2nd from right Dennis Parker and in the front row 2nd from the left is Bill Sparey. Frank Hancorn is far right on the front row.

CHAPTER VIII

Southern Villages

Many older cricketers will remember playing on uneven pitches in earlier days, thankfully not quite as bad as our cartoon depicts.

Tyberton Cricket Club

Left: A Photo of Tyberton Cricket Club, and an unknown visiting team, probably an invitation XI. The match was played at Stoney Field, Tyberton on the 28 August 1937.

The team was greatly influenced by the Lee Warner family who were the descendants of the Brydges family from Tyberton Court. They provided the umpire and a member of the home side. The umpires were Major C.B. Lee Warner and Rev E.H. Beattie; the scorer was Miss Joan Burney. Tyberton scored 80 and the visitors 61.

The visiting team back row left to right: H. Adams (Hay) G. Evans (Whitbourne), P. Evans (Whitbourne), J. Lee Warner (London), R. Burney (Hay), M. Adams (Hay).
Second row right to left: A. Roper (Hereford), V. Weaver (Blakemere), B. Wall, (Blakemere)
Front Row left to right: D. Spry (Preston), A. Williams (Preston).

An early photograph of **Longhope** Cricket Team taken outside their old pavilion in 1930.

The Longhope team in 1973

Back row left to right: Percy Yemm, Maurice Watkins, Gerald Wyman, Geoff Gurney, Harold Gurney, Sylvia Yemm (scorer).

Front row left to right: Ashley Hornchurch, Ian Stewart, Graham Ferguson, John Yemm, Gordon Cruickshank, Chris Yemm (aged 3).

CRICKET CLUB
FOUNDED 1897

Brockhampton cricket ground is nestled between two old wooded areas on a private estate; it is one of the most picturesque grounds in the county. The club have recently completed probably the most attractive clubhouse in the county. It also boasts a permanent marquee for corporate entertaining and sports evenings.

BROCKHAMPTON CRICKET CLUB

Summer Cricket Ball

Friday 18 June 2004
7.30pm for 8.00pm

Live band
Black tie

Tickets £25.00
including food

Brockhampton
Cricket Club Ground
The Parks
Brockhampton

Brockhampton new clubhouse was the brainchild of Roy Wargen, ably assisted by David Howells, with much help from other members. The club celebrated the opening by organising its first summer ball in 2004.

Roy Wargen joined Brockhampton in 1974 as a young raw fast bowler, but with some wise words and nurturing from experienced players like Tony Hope he developed into a fine accurate medium pace bowler. During this time Roy captained the club for long periods and he has been chairman since 1992. The club, after many promotions in recent years, played their first Birmingham league game in 2008. Another first for Brockhampton was when they hosted the first ever Birmingham league match between two Herefordshire clubs when they entertained Kington in the first match of the 2008 season.

The Brockhampton side that won the Highnam six-a-side competition in 1959.

Back Row left to right: Bert Howells, Tony Hope, David Hope.

Front row left to right: M. Hawkes, Gerald Howells, E. Williams.

Roy Wargen is pictured having a drink with friends after playing a match for Lang Lang, an Australian side.

In 1993 Roy decided to spend the year in Australia. He and a friend Paul Hodges went to Sydney where they were hoping to meet up with Max Chambers from the Manley Waratas. However due to unfortunate circumstances they missed each other. They went to find work as planned in the Melbourne area where they met Murray Walcott who became a close friend. Murray was a leg break bowler who played for a local club called Lang Lang. Having found work on a local farm Roy was accepted in to the Lang Lang Club after a few choice Pommie cracks to test his character. The season Roy was with them proved to be successful and they went on to win their first cup competition. Twenty years later Murray and his family came to England on a travelling holiday and called on Roy. He played twice for Brockhampton before moving on.

Brockhampton Cricket Club in 1980.
Runners up in League Division 1.

Back row left to right: Robin Williams, Tony Hope, Roy Wargen, Robin Hood, Vernon Hope, Kevin Williams.
Front Row left to right: Ted Amos, Steven Howells, John Burgoyne, Bill Harris, Gerald Howells.
Inset: Ray Evans captained the side for 9 seasons during the 1960s and 1980s.

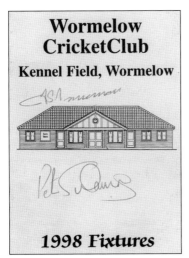

Wormelow CricketClub
Kennel Field, Wormelow

1998 Fixtures

Above: The fixture card for the first match played in 1998 between Wormelow and a representative XI to celebrate the opening of the new pavilion at Wormelow. Freddie Trueman, the former England and Yorkshire fast bowler, who performed the opening ceremony and National Hunt Jockey Peter Scudamore who played for the representative XI signed the card.

Right: **Richard Prime**, the Hereford Times sports editor is standing in front of the Wormelow old Pavilion just before it was demolished.

Bryngwyn Manor

The team at **Wormelow** originally went under the name of Bryngwyn CC. They are recorded in the local newspapers as playing between 1904 and the start of the First World War. The club was formed by Sir James Rankin who owned and lived at Bryngwyn Manor and was the Member of Parliament for Leominster and gave the town the Rankin Club. He also gifted Hereford City with the Museum and Library.

Wormelow CC then started playing in the early 1930s when Mrs Amy Simmonds, the local racehorse owner, was President and main benefactor. At this time the ground called 'The Park Field' was shared with the South Herefordshire Hunt Cricket Team and was on the Bryngwyn Manor estate.

Dave Sharland played for Wormelow in the 1940s before moving on to become captain of Harewood End CC. Dave's father also played for Wormelow and the South Herefordshire Hunt in the 1930s.

The start of a new era for Wormelow as they re-lay their wicket in 1964. Pictured leaning on his spade is Dave Verry; Colin Edmonds is using the rotovator, whilst club grounds man Tom Cooke is manoeuvring the wheelbarrow.
Unfortunately the fourth person cannot be recognised.

Wormelow in June 1998
Invitation Match to celebrate the opening of the new pavilion.

Above: **Wormelow**
Back row left to right: Nigel Evans, Tom Herbert, Andy Waring, Richard Gummery, Brian Pederson, Handley Scudamore Jnr.
Front row left to right: Ian Herbert, Henry Langford, Derry Porter, Shaun Waldron, Jamie Langford.

Below: **Invitation XI**
Back row left to right: Robbie Symons, Duncan Verry, Richard Evans, Ken Hook, Roy Wargen, Peter Scudamore.
Front row left to right: David Edmunds, Garth Lawson, Richard Prime, Peter Sykes, Stewart Gilbert.

Brampton Abbotts about 1937/8
(winners of an unknown trophy)
Back row left to right: Geoff Broad, Alan Matthews, Eric Morris, Bob Matthews, Dick Swivell, Raymond Hill, Fred Goode, Rev. Blakelock (umpire).
Front row left to right: Colin Goode (Scorer), Bill Steadman, Jack Whittaker, Alan Matthews (Captain), Charles Goode, Guy Sainsbury.

The Goode family played a major part at Brampton Abbotts cricket club in the 1930s. It is recorded that Brampton won the Perrystone cup in 1933 (right). Charles, Fred and Colin all played for the village and Christine (now Davies) acted as scorer for ten years until she moved to Solihull in 1947.

The pavilion at Brampton Abbotts was moved from the grove meadow and given to Bob Mawson by Norman Snell in 1975. It has survived and is still in the garden of Kath Mawson who is Bob's daughter.

Goodrich Cricket Club

In 1909 Lady Moffat, who resided at Goodrich Court, was a great benefactor of the Goodrich team and this historic photograph shows her with the team after she had presented them with her own challenge cup to be competed for by local teams each year.

Garway Cricket Club playing at Goodrich in 1910 (winning the Goodrich Cup).
Back row left to right: Rodger J. Lloyd, William Millham, (unknown person from Goodrich Court), J. Hughes, George Smith, and Albert Pritchard.
Front row left to right: Tom Benjamin, Ida C Millham, John James (Garway Schoolmaster), Lady Moffatt of Goodrich Court, Mr. Scully of Glenmonnow, lady from Goodrich Court, Harry Hemming.
Sitting left to right: Mr. Bowen, butler to Mr Scully.
A historic photograph showing R. J. Lloyd (Father to Douglas Lloyd), I. C. Millham (his mother) and William Millham (maternal grandfather). Photo supplied by Douglas Lloyd, who was headmaster of Norton Cross School.

Blanches

The old Blanches pavilion as it stands today

The fixture list for the previous year confirms that Jack Wadelin, who was the landlord of the Wye Inn at Rotherwas for many years, was club captain. His son Neil, who also played cricket, has followed his father in the licensing trade and is the current landlord of the Grafton Inn, Ross Road.

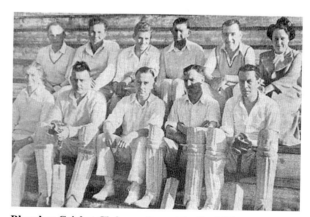

Blanches Cricket Club was formed by Cyril Blanche from Green Crize. This photo is of the team who had a successful season in Division 2 of the Hereford Evening League in 1952.

Back row, left to right: Cyril Blanche, B. White, M. Joseph, C. Nixon, R. Rowberry, Mrs. C. Nixon (scorer).

Front row left to right: D. Thomas, G. Farr, G. Armitage (captain), L. Copeland, F. Lewis.

Dymock were formed in 1868 and their first pavilion was a chicken hut. Geographically they are situated on the Hereford & Gloucester border but play most of their cricket in Herefordshire.

Above: An early 20th century photo of Dymock Cricket Club with an interesting top-hatted gentleman front middle.

Dymock 1980s
Back row:
Frank Miles, Keith Bishop, T Goulding, G Darley, D Bakewell, D Twigg.
Front row:
P Morgan, Les Darker, H (Chippy) Davies, M Smith, Tony Hehir.

The late Frank Miles who was Chairman of Hereford United Football Club when they attained Football League status for the first time is on the top left of this photograph, also in the photograph are Keith Bishop from Holme Lacy Cricket Club, Les Darker from Ross and Tony Hehir formerly of Hoarwithy. Tony became an umpire when he ceased playing.

Perrystone Court cricket team 1946

The picture shows the team with the Brockhampton & Perrystone Cups, which they had just won.

Back row left to right: Dennis Manning, Alan Teague, Bill Steadman, Fred Sollars, James Roberts, John Clinton, Ted Lerigo.

Middle row left to right: Harry Davies, Stan Young, Ivor Jones, Jack Davies.

Front row left to right: n/k, Trevor Manning.

Woolhope six-a-side

Bill Hodges   Norman Williams   Terry Preece   ? Potter   ? Williams   Brian Hoyes

Goodrich Cricket Club circa 1900

The distinguished gentleman with the large beard is arguably W G Grace?

Golden Valley 1950

Back row L-R: Glyn Williams; Bert Welsby; Jack Johnson; Guy Goring; Frank Shufflebotham; Cecil Williams; Ken Carter; Mr Shufflebotham (Umpire); David Oxynham.
Front row L-R: Don Thomas; Eddie Phillips; Owen Davies; Mrs B Welsby (Scorer); Elwyn Jones; Jack Davies; John Deville.

CHAPTER IX

Northern Villages

Cartoon depicting a typical village cricket match.

A NEAR THING.

Disappointed Trundler. "NEARLY 'AD 'E, JARGE."   *Disappointed Batsman.* "AH, AN' NEARLY 'IT 'E!"

Docklow Cricket Club about 1955
Ernie and George Preston who owned Docklow Manor, formed Docklow Cricket Club in the early 1950s. The team played on the estate in Park Field. The photo shows the players with their trophies after winning the Orleton league in about 1955. Team members playing in this era were Ernie and George Preston, Bob and Jim Vickress, the four Gwynne brothers, two Leggs and two Williams brothers.
The Manor was sold to Beastons of Shrewsbury in 1973 and cricket ceased. The pavilion was sold to Burghill and Tillington Cricket Club for £12.50p. Some of the Docklow players formed a team at the Downs, Bromyard.
(Photograph by Malcolm Ormerod)

Withington Cricket Club was formed around the turn of the 20th century and were very strong during their first decade when the Dent family were very supportive on and off the playing field.

The sign of the Cross Keys at Withington (The team's Logo)

Withington CC joined the Hereford and District cricket league in 1922, just two years after the league began. In 1921 the chairman of the league invited the club to join, subject to improving their facilities. The club engaged in a fundraising campaign like never before: all the vice-presidents were contacted and a concerted effort was made to find new ones. A grand draw, concert and dances were also arranged; the draw made £20 and the concert £10, which was sufficient to invite a Mr Wood to submit an estimate for the relaying of the cricket square. Mr. Wood suggested that he could do the job for £2-10s per week plus 15s for a boy to assist, and he considered that it would take about eight weeks to complete the work. It was also suggested that the club should look for a suitable pavilion.

In 1928 the club bought some new kit from Hatton Bros and Perks, outfitters: namely an autographed bat at 33s, a cannon bat 25s, a pair of batting gloves 6s, two pairs of leg guards 3s, three balls 27s, one scorebook 2s and two handle grips at 2s. It was also recommended that the club should employ a full time groundsman, and Mr. Fred Brown was duly appointed at a salary of 50s per season. The subscriptions were 2/6d per annum and the treasurers report for the year showed the club had a balance of £13-17s-9d. Withington were very fortunate to have a strong enthusiastic committee and membership during the 1920s and 30s including the Rev. Reed, George Norton, W.G. Farmer, A.R.W. Skip, S. Saxby, F. Morgan, W. Carver, Mr. Godsell, J. Davies, T.J. Hawkins, Mr. Borage, J.H. Clarke, M.B. Parry-Jones and Thomas Watkins. Harry Wragg became a vice president of the club in 1932 and saw his sons David, T and L Wragg play for the club in 1942.

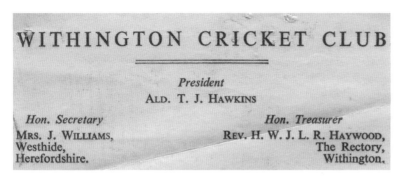

Withington cricket club headed notepaper in 1950.
(Photo courtesy of John Hall)

Withington circa 1960.
Back row, left to right: Bill Tinton, John Hall, Ray Norton (secretary/treasurer), David Grindle, Howard Staples, John Peters, Brian Price.
Middle row left to right: John Clarke, Philip Price (Captain), Ken Pilliner, Charlie Cooper.
Front row left to right: Don Phillips, George Hill. (Photo by Philip Price)

The photograph *(left)* shows the players in 1960 when Philip Price, Ray Norton and John Hall played a major part in running the team.

The Cross Keys, formerly Withington, team in 2006

Standing left to right: A. Powell, T. Baker, H. Cooke, M. Stobbs, B. Darby, D. Ford.
Sitting left to right: J. Verdin, S. Dent, P. Kirby, H. Powles, A. Marson.
Front: Hattie the dog, N. Dent.

Alan Roberts is a long-standing umpire and secretary of
Bringsty Cricket Club. He is a member of the Herefordshire
and Worcestershire umpires association.

BRINGSTY CRICKET CLUB

FIXTURE CARD SEASON 1964

President :
E. Y. Robinson, Esq.

Chairman : L. Essenhigh, Esq.

Captain : C. G. Essenhigh, Esq.

Vice-Captain E. Hawkins, Esq.

Hon. Secretary : E. Hawkins, Esq.

Hon. Treasurer : C. G. Essenhigh, Esq.

Hon. Match Secretary : E. Hawkins, Esq.

Hon. Auditor : F. Clements, Esq.

Groundsman : D. Hall, Esq.

Committee :
Officers Ex-Officio with Messrs L. Goulding,
E. Oliver, R. Powell, B. Powell, B. Turner,
J. Bowlcott, C. Turner, W. Norris.

Bringsty Tea Time
Photograph of a typical village cricket family gathering at tea time. One of the
tea ladies for many years was Phyllis Essenhigh the wife of Les, and mother of
Gwyn, Donald and David all of whom played for the club in the late 1950s and
1960s. The pavilion is in the background.

Bringsty Fixture card for 1964
David Essenhigh played for Bringsty until
he was 15. He then became a professional
apprentice on the Lords ground staff
during which time he played a number of
games for the MCC. Whilst at Lords he
started a coaching course, before taking
up a coaching position with Marlborough
college. David eventually went on to play
for Wiltshire County Cricket Club. He now
lives in Cheltenham where he continues
playing and coaching at the age of 71.

Bringsty Cricket Club dinner and dance, which was held at the Talbot Hotel,
Knightwick in 1957. The club won the Leominster Knock Out Cup that year.

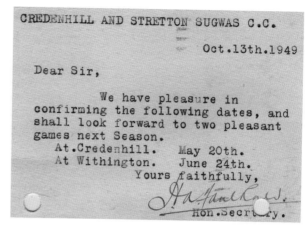

CREDENHILL AND STRETTON SUGWAS C.C.

Oct.13th.1949

Dear Sir,

We have pleasure in confirming the following dates, and shall look forward to two pleasant games next Season.
At.Credenhill.   May 20th.
At Withington.   June 24th.
Yours faithfully,

Hon.Secretary.

Credenhill & Stretton Sugwas Cricket Club
In 1949 the club arranged home and away matches against Withington. The note above is typewritten long before the days of email or fax. The note also confirms the existence then of two teams who no longer exist.

Credenhill wicketkeeper Terry Strange crouched ready for action. The old Credenhill pavilion is in the background.

Burley Gate team in the 1960s.
Back row left to right: Ray Jones, Alan Jones, ? Weaver, Mike Tidmarsh, John Bowler, Brian Draper.
Front row left to right: George Price, Ken Watson (?), Eric Bayliss, Dave Frost, John Arnett, Ray Hince.
During this period Jean Tidmarsh recalled preparing the cricket teas with Sheila Hince and Flossy Bayliss. Ray and Sheila Hince have supported the club throughout its existence. (Photograph courtesy of Mike Tidmarsh)

Lyonshall Cricket Club were the winners of the Kingsland & Presteigne Knock Out competition in 1938.

Back row left to right: Robbie Richardson, H. James, W. G. Ellson.
Middle row left to right: T. Boore, E. Roberts, J. L. Morgan, H. Pennell, J. Ruff, R. H. Bromley.
Front row left to right: R. Munslow, R. Burgoyne, F. G. Burgoyne, F. S. Bromley, P. Burgoyne, R. Mainwaring, W. Jones.

Robbie Richardson later played an important part in the life of Kington Cricket Club. The team also includes three members of the local Burgoyne family who still run a marquee and haulage business in Lyonshall and continue to play and sponsor cricket locally.

In 1937 Fred Burgoyne took 10 wickets for 5 runs and helped bowl out Eardisley for 12 runs. On another occasion in 1939 Lyonshall beat Kington after bowling them out for 46. The only evidence for a team at Lyonshall is in the 1930s.

Orleton Cricket Club in 1956.
The photo is of the team who beat Eyton in the local knockout cup.

Back row from left to right: Michael Sparey, Mick Cadwallader, John Evans, Desmond Fortey, Michael Ball, Dick Tipton.

Front row: Alan Wall, Roy Gittings, Jim Collings, George Morgan, John Lewis.

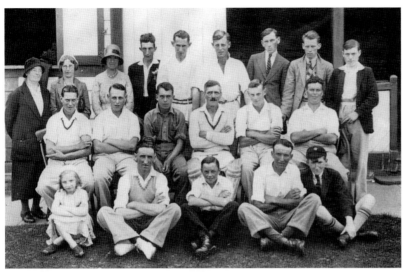

Titley Cricket Club played first in 1859 on a ground at Dinehill on the Titley Court Estate. The picture is from circa 1930 outside Kington Pavilion.
Back row left to right: Mrs. Brickley, Florrie Brickley, Mrs. Lloyd, Bill Turner, Bob Burgoyne, Fred Burgoyne, Ronnie Diggory, Cyril Lloyd, Jack Bufton.
Middle row left to right: Tom Davies, Harry James, Charlie Lloyd, Jim Ruff, Jack James, Henry Mills.
Front row left to right: n/k, Ernie Lloyd, Wesley Jones, Frank Mills, Jack Christopher.

Above: The scorecard of a match between Titley and Shobdon played at Titley in 1929.

Left: The **Teale** family are stalwarts of Shobdon CC. The photograph shows father Terry in the middle with sons Matthew on the left and Andrew right. Terry's wife Pat has been a club scorer for many years and a keen supporter of the club.

Above: **Shobdon Cricket Club** dinner dance to raise funds for the Pavilion. Colonel V. Corbett *(right)* presented cups to the top bowler and batsman of the 1961 season who were Ernie Smith *(left)* and Ken Evans *(centre)*. The photograph is regrettably poor but the only one known of this occasion.

A typical 1930s teatime at a village cricket match under the oak tree at **Shobdon**.

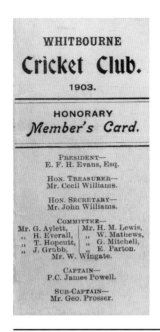

Whitbourne team in 1923

*Back Row left to right: L. Matthews Snr. (umpire) R.Jones,
C.Smith, C.Williams, J.Vernalls,
J. Mitchell, J. Grub (umpire).
Front row left to right: F. Green (Scorer),
J. Tomkins, W. Matthews, C. Robinson,
W. Mitchell, Capt. E.F.H. Evans,
W. Griffiths, E.H. Griffiths.*
NB. Ian Botham *(right)* was the President
1990 whilst playing for Worcestershire.

Harewood End cricket ground.

There is an unconfirmed story that one of the landowners of Harewood Park went on to the mound with his new bride for a picnic, where she apparently lost her wedding ring. They hunted high and low for it without success. He therefore planted the ring of poplar trees around the area and said that the ground must not be ploughed up in his lifetime unless the ring was found. There is no evidence that it ever has.

After the Second World War a local cricket team was formed and it was decided to turn the area into a cricket ground. The club members dug out the pitch area and Godfrey Davies, the local farmer, and one of his workmen Cyril Barnfield laid the concrete strip, which can still be seen today. The club continued playing into the early 1990s after which the old pavilion stood unused until 1996. The photo, taken early in 2006 (below), shows the old building in a sad state of repair, shortly before it was demolished.

Below: Panorama of Stoke Edith House
Right: Copy OS map showing position of Stoke Edith cricket ground.

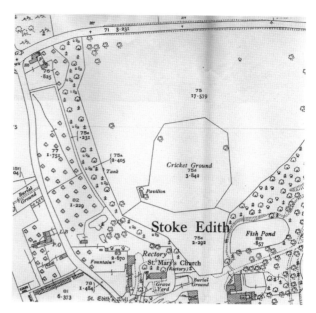

Frome Valley circa 1950.

The Frome Valley/Stoke Edith cricket club ceased when Andrew Foley, son of Tom Foley inherited the estate. He informed the club that he required the cricket field for agricultural purposes and was not prepared to accept that because the ground had been in use as a cricket ground for the majority of the 20th century, that it should be preserved for the game. The events leading up to the demise of the club are recorded in detail in the minutes of the club, which have survived.

Frome Valley team photo taken on the 10th August 1929

Back Row left to right: H.C. Dent, H. Higgins, F.J. Tolley, C. Griffiths, H.Webley, H.A. Picton. (Hon. sec).
Front Row left to right: F. Morgan, H.R. Griffiths, W.F. Watson, P.E. Bradstock, C.W.F. Pudge, I. Bond, J.N.F. Vale.

Frome Valley team in 1957
Back row left to right: Mike Tidmarsh, A. J. Holland, Peter A. Davies, L. Jones, Sir John Foley, Mike Built.
Front row left to right: Eddie Collins, P. H. Foley, Reverend Steele, Tom Bradstock, Ron Bishop.

Trevor Jones recalls, during a cricket match played in the 1960s, when a young man was batting for Garnons on the coconut matting wicket. There was a tremendous rainstorm, but the wicket was not affected and the game continued. However, the batsman's mother, being over-concerned for her son, walked into the game with an umbrella, held it over his head and said "come on darling we are going home otherwise you will catch a dreadful cold".

The Garnons team that won the Pavilion Sports Cup for the second year running by beating the Bulmer's team at Wormelow in 2001 by 133 runs. This secured successive league Division 1 and cup doubles. Andy Brace was top scorer with 77 not out.

Back row left to right: Steve Newton, Trevor Jones, Jim Cotterell, Alun Jones, Dave Knight, Danny Gomberra.

Front row left to right: Dave Brown, John Andrews, Andy Brace, Rob Pritchard, Brian Pugh, Stuart Griffiths.

Garnons/St. Mary's in August 1982 taken at Bromyard.
Back row left to right: Tim Coleman, Molly Jones (scorer), Stuart Blake, John McGeevor, Val Treagus, David Phillips, Andy Chambers.
Front row left to right: John Wade, Ian Ferguson, Trevor Jones (captain.), Kevin Hoey, Brian Taylor.

Colwall is one of he oldest Cricket Clubs in Herefordshire. The club was formed in 1839 and initially they played friendly matches. Many first class cricketers have played for and appeared at the club during the last century.

Below: A letter to Adrian Berry from Ricardo Ellcock, the Barbados-born England First Class cricketer.

Colwall: two generations of the Berry family.
Back row left to right: brothers Phil, Fred and George.
Front row left to right: brothers Kim, Adrian and Jonathon.

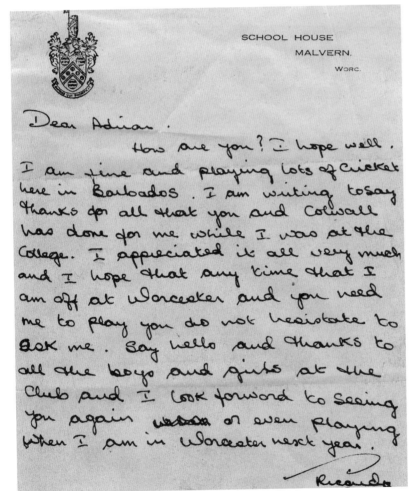

Adrian Berry proudly holding the Three Counties League winners shield for Colwall in 1982.

Photograph of friends and club mates Jim Sandford and the late John Taylor smiling proudly as they collected a trophy on their way to joint dental appointments!

Back row left to right: Bill Jenkins, Fred Mills, Baron Taylor, Jim Powell, Ada Winter, Edward Bill, Ron Onions, Reg Baldwin, Mr. Elliott.
Front row left to right: Den Berry, Gerald Davies, Harold Kitchen, Ted Winter, Bill Howells.

Canon Frome

There are newspaper reports confirming that Canon Frome were playing in the early part of the last century. The inaugural meeting of the club however was not held until 1938 at the Hopton Arms. Henry Haywood chaired the meeting. The team's first games were played at Mainstone Court with the permission of the Reverend Toynbee. Canon Frome have been very successful over the years and the current side is maintaining the clubs high standard.

Brian Goode, and George Whittaker leaving the old club pavilion at Wassington.

Canon Frome circa 1980

Back row left to right: George Whittaker, Charlie Barnett, Roger Helme, John Evans, Neil Andrews, Des Samuels.
Front row left to right: Tony Beale, Chris Styles, Mike Sterry, Maurice Emburey, Brian Goode.

Canon Frome circa 1970

Back row left to right: Maurice Emburey, Ron Franklin, Edward Davies, John Griffiths, Jack Whittaker, Bob Thirkle, Ian Barnes, Harry Pudge.

Front row left to right: John Evans, Dick Whittaker, Brian Goode, Ivor Hunt, George Whittaker.

Burghill & Tillington cup winning team 2007

Back row left to right: Ian Graham, Steve de Souza, Kingsley Morris, Mark Preece, Peter Eames, Tim Walsh, Mike Pledge, Alex Hedges, Dave Knight.

Front row: Les Gibson, John Terry, Neil Box (Captain), Edward Oliver, Matthew Biggs.

The team won the Marches League Cup by beating Goodrich by 94 runs at Brockhampton. This was a fine performance with Kingsley Morris scoring 137 not out off 109 balls and Alex Hedges 136 runs off 89 balls. They shared an opening partnership of 227 and this was their third 200 partnership of the season.

Burghill & Tillington late 1980s
Photograph includes Brian Tutchenor, Managing Director of Plastic Injection Mouldings who sponsored the club for many years, with grateful members of the team who were affectionately known as "Beastie Boys".

L-R Duncan (doughnut) Sparrow, Ian Eyre, Ken Hook, Jeremy (Jumbo) Symonds, Simon (Wally) Wilton, Alan (Edger) Edge, Carl (Rosie) Rose, Kevin (KGB) Bayliss.
Front row: Mike (Stanner) Stanley, Brian Tutchenor, Ian Macklin.

Burghill & Tillington Cricket Club 1975

Standing left to right Crawford Perkins, Mason Helme (President), Stan Nicholls, Dave Griffiths, D. Owen, B. Beavan.

Sitting left to right Rodney Lodge, Richie Downes, Len Sparrow, Ian Macklin, John Downes, Des Lawrence.
(Photograph Vivien of Hereford)

In 1975 Mason Helme gave permission for the Brick House field to be used as a cricket ground for the foreseeable future. Mrs Desiree Helme followed on after Mason died and the club are very grateful to the family for their generosity.

CHAPTER X

Past Cricket Teams and Grounds

During the 20th century many cricket teams and grounds in Herefordshire have been lost. The County supported many more village clubs than today, and also a thriving Evening League Competition. Sadly many of these clubs have now ceased playing.

This has followed a national trend as cricket competes with other interests. Many of the grounds still have visible evidence of their existence. Others are known about because of information held in the local record office and library. For some of these clubs the authors have found old photographs and ephemera, which are included in *Cricket in Herefordshire in the 20th Century* which was published in 2007 or in other chapters in this book. Where this has not been possible they are referred to here.

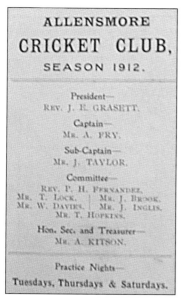

A 1912 card for the long lost Allensmore Cricket Club.

Cyril Blanche, a local businessman who ran his own cricket team at Green Crize, Hereford.

The 1948 fixture list for Credenhill & Sugwas Cricket Club.

SUTTON & DISTRICT SPORTS CLUB

President : Mr. S. C. ANDREWS
Chairman : Rev. W. R. THOMAS
Captain : Mr. P. BAILES

(CRICKET SECTION)

Gen. Secretary : Mr. R. J. REYNOLDS
Match Secretary : Mr. H. MILLICHAP,
School House, Sutton, Hereford.
Phone : Sutton St. Nicholas 203.

The notepaper heading for the Sutton & District Sports Club cricket section in 1952.

Left: The **Staunton-on-Arrow** cricket team, date unknown.

Back row left to right: Fred Thomas and Richard Edwards. Middle row left to right: n/k, n/k, John Edwards, David Griffiths, n/k.

Front row left to right: Richard Edwards Jnr, David Sayers, n/k, Ken Griffiths.

BURLEY GATE CRICKET CLUB

Headquarters: BURLEY GATE INN, HEREFORD

President: T. GUMMER, Esq.

Hon. Sec. W. J. Bowler.

Phone: BURLEY GATE 211

Headed notepaper for **Burley Gate Cricket Club**. The headquarters were the local pub!

Staunton-on-Wye Cricket Club was formed originally in 1859 and is recorded again in the early 1900s and then in the 1930s. The photo shows the old cricket pavilion when the side played on land owned by Mr. Pearson Gregory. The team folded around 1960 and the football team took over the building.

Photograph taken in 2006 of a sad former Golden Valley pavilion.

Holme Lacy

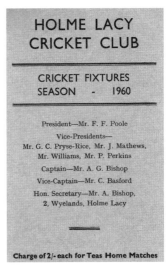

HOLME LACY
CRICKET CLUB

CRICKET FIXTURES
SEASON - 1960

President—Mr. F. F. Poole

Vice-Presidents—
Mr. G. C. Pryse-Rice, Mr. J. Mathews,
Mr. Williams, Mr. P. Perkins

Captain—Mr. A. G. Bishop

Vice-Captain—Mr. C. Basford

Hon. Secretary—Mr. A. Bishop,
2, Wyelands, Holme Lacy

Charge of 2/- each for Teas Home Matches

Holme Lacy pavilion. This was formerly the pavilion at Hoarwithy (see remains below).   Holme Lacy fixture card 1960.

Hoarwithy

All that remain are the foundations of the Hoarwithy pavilion.

YMCA were one of the first eight teams to form the original Hereford and District cricket league in 1920. They won the first ever game played in the league by beating Wye Valley by 119 runs on the 15th May. In the same year YMCA went on to win the league and also the Hereford Times Challenge Shield beating Frome Valley in the final.

Telephone No.: CAREY 205   10539

J. B. & O. TOPPING
Grocery, Provisions and Newsagents
THE STORES
HOARWITHY, HEREFORD

M. Hoarwithy Cricket Club 26-8-1967

1	½ Serviettes 2/6 Dish Cloth 1/1	3	7
2	Sm Vinegar 1/2 ~ HAD 5/8/67	1	2
3	Afternoon Tea "Serviettes" HAD 19/8/67	1	10
4			
5	2 Sugar	1	6
6	½ Tea	1	6
7	½ cheese	1	11
8	Tin Salmon	3	1
9	½ Tomatoes	1	4
10	1 onion		4½
11	6 eggs	1	11½
12	1 fruit cake 2/6 1 Angel Cake 2/4	4	10
13	1 Madera cake	2	2
14	2 Pints Milk	1	8
15	1 Tin Milk	1	5
16	11B Magic Magazine	2	5
17		£1-10-9	

The ivy has taken over the former Moreton and Lyde pavilion, which is now being used as a games room for a camping site.

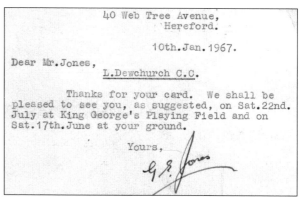

A note from the secretary of Little Dewchurch Cricket Club to Burley Gate in 1967. Little Dewchurch were playing their home games on the King George V1 playing fields in Hereford because by this date their own ground had been built on.

Right: Headed note dated 1926 for **Rowden Abbey** Cricket Club. The letter was to a firm of local solicitors regarding the lease on their ground.

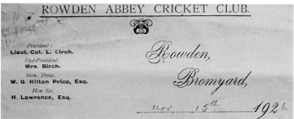

MORETON AND LYDE CRICKET CLUB
FIXTURES FOR 1974

President—P. J. Meredith, Esq.
Chairman—H. Perkins, Esq.
Vice-Chairman—B. Lambert, Esq.
Captain of Club—V. Jones, Esq.
Tel. : Hereford 2253
Vice-Captain of Club—John Griffiths, Esq.

Vice-Presidents

C. Blanch, Esq.	B. Moore, Esq.
C. D. Davies, Esq.	E. Moreton, Esq.
J. Davies, Esq.	C. Perkins, Esq.
C. Foden, Esq.	H. Perkins, Esq.
L. Hoddell, Esq.	A. A. Price, Esq.
C. Knipe, Esq.	R. Pomeroy, Esq.
B. G. Lambert, Esq.	R. Probert, Esq.
J. M. Langford, Esq.	E. J. Rees, Esq.
H. Lyke, Esq.	J. Rees, Esq.
W. Makin, Esq.	G. Rosser, Esq.
R. C. Manning, Esq.	G. O. Sainsbury, Esq.
P. J. Meredith, Esq.	D. R. Bishop, Esq.

General Secretary—C. H. Foden, Esq.
Chaveron, Moreton-on-Lugg
Tel. : Burghill 287
Hon. Treasurer—F. Perkins, Esq.
Upper House, Moreton. Tel. : Burghill 245
Fixture Secretary—W. J. Jackson, Esq.
3, Broad Street, Leominster. Tel. 3401

The 1974 fixture list for Moreton and Lyde Cricket Club. The fixture secretary was Bill Jackson, a local estate agent, and the treasurer was the late Francis Perkins.
Included in the list of vice-presidents is Cyril Blanche who also ran his own cricket team.

One of the most hotly contested competitions between the two World Wars was the Perrystone Cup, donated by Sir Sidney Clive of Perrystone Court. The Perrystone team played on a ground at the Court.

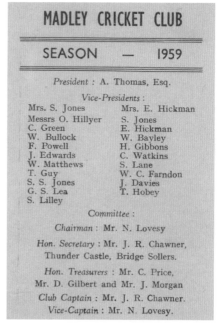

MADLEY CRICKET CLUB

SEASON — 1959

President : A. Thomas, Esq.

Vice-Presidents :

Mrs. S. Jones	Mrs. E. Hickman
Messrs O. Hillyer	S. Jones
C. Green	E. Hickman
W. Bullock	W. Bayley
F. Powell	H. Gibbons
J. Edwards	C. Watkins
W. Matthews	S. Lane
T. Guy	W. C. Farndon
S. S. Jones	J. Davies
G. S. Lea	T. Hobey
S. Lilley	

Committee :

Chairman : Mr. N. Lovesy

Hon. Secretary : Mr. J. R. Chawner,
Thunder Castle, Bridge Sollers.

Hon. Treasurers : Mr. C. Price,
Mr. D. Gilbert and Mr. J. Morgan

Club Captain : Mr. J. R. Chawner.

Vice-Captain : Mr. N. Lovesy.

Madley Cricket Club fixture card for 1959. There were enough vice-presidents to form their own team!

Hampton Court

Right: When the Arkwrights moved from Hampton Court to Kinsham they continued the Arkwright cricket tradition. This Photograph is of the 1931 Kinsham team. Some team members have been identified, they are as follows:

Back row left to right: Sir John Arkwright, Billy Beavan, n/k. Alan Morgan, Arthur Rogers, John Garstone, n/k, David Edwards, Frank Chilman.

Front row left to right: Frank Edwards, n/k, Jack Dyke, Mr. Garstone, Harry Price.

The pavilion shown in the background is unusual, in that it is octagonal and it is believed that it was based on a municipal building in Tenbury Wells.

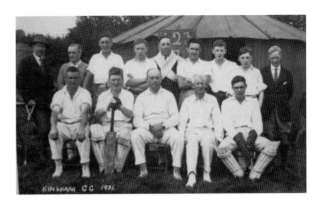

Bodenham Cricket Club reformed in 1890 at Bodenham Court Farm. The photo shows some well-known personalities of the time including J.S. Arkwright from Hampton Court (on the rear left wearing a cap); Dr. Hall, a club vice president (centre front); Mr. Williams, the local schoolmaster (standing behind Dr. Hall) and Mr. Dean, the future schoolmaster.

Pontrilas Cricket Club circa 1930s
Reg Michael was secretary at this time and also continued in that post when Pontrilas merged and played under Ewyas Harold CC in the early 1950s, where he continued to officiate until his death.

Both photo's supplied by Tom Morgan of Ewyas Harold garage.

A fun cricket match played at Pontrilas before the 2nd World War.

Nash Rocks

Nash Rocks Cricket team 1930

Nash Rocks quarry, near Yardro, ran a cricket team before the Second World War. Joe Lane is on the far left standing. He was still in the cup winning team five years later (see below).

Nash Crushers 1935

Nash Rock Crushers who won the Knockout Cup in 1935.
Sitting in the front row left is Joe Lane who was uncle to June, the wife of Cedric Davies who played cricket for Wiggins in the 1980s. (Photo by Yates)

On 31 August 1905 the **Stoke Edith Ladies** played the Gents. The teams were
Mr. P. H. Foley's XI and Hon. Miss Leigh's XI. The fairer sex won by 8 runs (104 to 96).

P.H. Foley's XI. Back row, left to right: Mrs Foley, Miss Wilkinson, Mrs B. Davenport,
Miss Romilly, Miss Foster Hunt. Centre row: the Hon. C. Lyttelton, Revd C. Robinson,
H.K. Foster, ? Braithwaite, W.B. Burns, H. Bromley Davenport, A.M. Miller,
P. Bradstock. Front row: P. Foley, F.W. Romney, G. Robinson, W.S. Bird.

Cricket at Stoke Edith. These two photographs, by H. Pattison, record a famous match in
September 1907. This is the Hon. Miss Leigh's XI. Back row, left to right: Mrs Butler
D. Leigh, Revd Mr Leveson-Gower, Mrs Leigh, R.F. Bailey, H. Charrington, Dr Higgins
Centre row: G. Bosworth Smith, H.R.G. Leveson-Gower, G.A. Denny, E.G.M
Carmichael. Front row: G.G. Napier, J. Douglas, R.P. Keigwin, Captain Butler.

Westfields c.1970
Back row L-R: Eric Williams; Les Campbell; Phil Donovan; Taffy Davies; Angus McIntyre; Mick Cooper.

Front row L-R: Russell Jones; Keith Bullock; Chris Moore (Capt.); Ken Pole; Ken Hedley.

Herefordian Nomads c. late 1960s.
Back row L-R: Tracey Goodwin; James Knipe; John Gummery; Jim Sandford; P. Davies; Malcolm Hughes.

Front row L-R: Dave Entwhistle; Rodney Jarrett; Terry Morgan (Capt.); Dave Cloxton; Chris Moore.

Thynnes 1949
Thynnes Cricket Club were a very successful limited overs team in the 1940s and 1950s, winning many evening league and K/O cup honours. They were photographed at Widemarsh common after winning Division 2 of the Hereford evening league in 1949.

Back row: n/k, n/k, J Handley, n/k, n/k, W Jennings, G Kershaw, Reg Braide.

Front row: F Farmer, G Marchant, Ernie Ridger (Capt), V Haylings, R Ingram.

The Cross Keys emblem proudly depicted on Ray Norton's Withington
Cricket Club Cap.

Withington were a thriving cricket club in the early part of the 20th century when the Dent family were very much involved. H J Dent is on this 1904 postcard, he was a fine opening bowler who played for Herefordshire against Worcester Club and Ground in 1904. Simon Dent, who plays for Cross Keys, Withington, is the great grandson of H J Dent and can be seen on the photo in chapter 9. The other Dent family members playing are D J Dent (former Mayor of Leominster) and P Dent. Another interesting player was the Rev A E Green-Price who also played for Herefordshire and the Hereford Gents and later the Brecon Gents. The remaining members of the team are as follows H E Stonyer, C G Bosanquet, S Corbett, W Jansey, W H Edwards, A F Goodwin, C and H Morgan, A and H Hill and C and J Davies.

Water Board Cricket Team circa 1975
Back row L-R Sandy Woolridge, n/k, Barry Singleton, Phil Johnson, n/k, Tony Chambers.
Front row L-R Jack Richards, Ian Robinson, Roger Warley, Tony Barter, Mike Beveridge, Mike Bullough.
Colleen Rogers of Woolhope CC and England Ladies also played with the team in this era.

Burton Court cricket ground hosted the Herefordshire Militia team in June 1902. Note the path that runs through the middle of the cricket ground.

The following list is of many long since forgotten teams and, where possible, when they played.

Team	Dates	Team	Dates
All Saints	1921	Kings Pyon	Evidence in local press
Aymestry	1914	Kingsland	1910 to 1973
Birley Court	1910	Kinsham	1910 to 1953
Bishopstone	Dates unknown	Kynaston	1904 to 1910
Bishopswood	Pre 1900 to 1914	Lea	1950s to 1964
Bodenham	1890 to 1989	Ledbury Corn Traders	1921
Boundary CC	1950s	Ledbury Farmers	1921
Bowling Green	1925	Leominster Institute and Circle	Evidence in local press
Bradley Court	1904 to 1927	Linton	1956 to 1960
Brampton Abbotts	Post WW1 to 1962	Longhope	1886 to 1989
Brampton Bryan	1914 then 1921 to 1930	Lyonshall	1914 to 1930s
Bredenbury	Evidence in local press	Male Voice Choir	1929
Bridstow	1953 to 1966	Mansion House	1920 and 1921
Bringsty	1930s to 1990s	Merry Millers	1971 to 2000
Broomsgreen	1930s	Michael Church Eskley	Formed in the 1980s
Burghill Hospital	1904 to 1989	Monkland	1921 and 1951
Burley Gate	Late 1940s to 1967	Mordiford	1929 to 1931
Burton Court	1864 to 1939	Moreton and Lyde	1953 to 1974
Callow Wayfarers	1961 to 1964	Much Marcle	1920 to 1968
Canon Pyon	1913 to 1939	Municipal Officers Social Club	Unknown
Castle Green	1925	Odds and Ends	1938
Cradley	1910 and 1925 to 1929	Orleton	1947 to late 1950s
Crusaders	Played 1991 to 1994	Pembridge	1913 to 1975
Dilwyn	1938 to the 1950s	Penrhos	1925
Docklow	1951 to 1972	Peterchurch	1904 to early 1950s
Dowty Sports	Evidence in press	Play Centre	1921
Eignbrook	1920 to 1927	Red & White Bus Service	1931
English Bicknor	1920s & 1930s	Redhill	Evidence in local press
Forthampton	1914 and 1921	Ross Nomads	1970 to 1973
Frome Valley-Stoke Edith	1900 to 1969	Ross St. Mary's	Evidence in local press
Gamecock	1992 and 1993	Ryelands	1920
Garway	1900 to 1910	Sanitary Laundry	1936 to 1939
Gateway	Evening League 1985	Sellack	1950s to 1963
Greenlands	1910	Staunton on Arrow	Pre WW2 to 1951
Grosmont	1946	Staunton On Wye	1921 to 1964
Hairdressers Assistants	1910	Stoke Bishop	Evidence in local press
Hampton Court	1844 to 1910	Stoke Bliss	1921-1931 and 1953-1974
Hereford City Council	1929	Stoke Lacy	1903 and 1904
Hereford Club & Ground	1904 to 1909 and 1920	Stoke Prior	1937
Hereford Constitutional	1904 to 1910	Sutton St Nicholas	1947 to 1968
Hereford Early Closers	Early 1900s	Titley	1859 to 1977
Hereford Excelsiors	1904 to 1910	Town Hall Staff	Mid 1930s & during WW2
Hereford Fruit Co	1931	Tupsley & District Cricket Club	1913 and 1914
Hereford Labour Club	1929	Tyberton	1937 to 1950s
Hereford Liberal Club	1910 and 1925	Upton Bishop	1909 to 1961
Hereford Mens Club	1909 and 1910	Walford	1920 and 1921 also 1960s
Hereford Thistle	Late 19th & early 20th Cent	Wesleyan	1904
Hereford Times	1910. 1927 and 1961	West End	1904
Hereford United Supporters Club	1960s and 1970s	Westhide	Playing up to 1939 and in 1965
Herefordians Grafton	1984 to 2001	Weston	1900 to 1980s
Ivington	1920 to 1989	White Lion	1921
Kenchester	Early 1900s	Whitney	1909 to 1914 & 1920-1921
Kimbolton	1949 to 1964	Withington	1904 late 1960s
Kings Acre & Breinton	1909 1910 and 1925		
Kings Caple	1904		

CHAPTER XI

From Strength to Strength – into the future

Many clubs in Herefordshire have won their way through to play Worcester Crusader League and Birmingham League cricket over the past decade. The following are a few of those clubs. If cricket in Herefordshire continues improving at the same rate the future looks good!

Brockhampton Cricket Club

Brockhampton won Division three of the Birmingham & District League in 2008. The team were promoted from Division Three to Division Two in their maiden season in the League. The Club Chairman Roy Wargen stated that the success was due to a great effort by everyone in the club emphasising the coaching of Ed Price, the all round performance of Chris Burroughs and inspired captaincy of Jonny Walker.

Back Row left to right: Ed Price (Coach), Tom Austwick, Shaun Cartwright, Andy Watkins, Adam Hewlett, Henry Langford, Chris Burroughs.
Front Row left to right: Richard Parker, Roy Wargen (Chairman), Jonny Walker (Captain), Ashley Nahorniak, Nick Price, Nick Denny.

The modern-day pavilion and club house.

Eastnor Cricket Club

Eastnor CC is one of the County's most prestigious clubs. They had a fine season in 2008. They won the Crusader Worcester County League Division 1 title. This title won them promotion to the Birmingham and District Cricket League Division 3. The club also regularly host Minor Counties Cricket for Herefordshire Cricket Club.

Back Row: Roy Jones (umpire) Jim Sandford, Christian Ferreira, Shahid Ahmed, Stephen Hughes, Nick Bollom, Emlyn Vicarage, David James (umpire)
Front Row: Chalid Jabman, Haris Saleem, Maria Ferreira, Ashad Hussian, Nineem, Keith Fortey.

Burghill and Tillington updated 21st century pavilion.

Burghill & Tillington Cricket Club

Burghill won promotion to Division 3 of the Crusader Worcester County League in 2008 by finishing runners up in Division 4. They won the league play-off against Stourbridge 3rds.

The reason for the play-off was that Division 4 is divided into two parts, North and South. The top team in each get automatic promotion, the second placed teams have to play-off for the 3rd spot. The game was played at Tenbury Wells just one week after the town had been cut off by the flooding of a local brook, not the river as may have been expected.

As a result the ground was not in the best of condition as can be seen in the photo and the muddy state of the kit of the more active fielders in the side.

Les Gibson, the groundsman and umpire at Burghill, said that the club's success was helped by their New Zealand-born player Alex Hedges who scored 1200 runs at an average of 101 and chipped in with 28 wickets.

Back Row left to right: Steve De Souza, Mark Preece, Tim Walsh, Kingsley Morris, Alex Hedges, Mike Pledge.
Front Row left to right: Ed Oliver, Neil Box (Captain), Matt Biggs, John Terry, Peter Eames.

Colwall Cricket Club

In 2008 Colwall were promoted to Division 1 of the Crusader Worcester County League,
after winning the Division 2 title.

Back row L-R: Tim Riley, Tom Wolfendale, Charlie Griffiths, Damien Berry, Nick Kontarines (scorer), Odge Davey, Mat King.
Front row L-R: Nick Panniers, Ed Smith, Mike King (Captain), Pete Butler, Ben Wheeler.

The main contributors to this successful season were Charlie Griffiths (bowling) and Nick Panniers with the bat.

There were two other notable successes in the County in 2008. Kington were successfully maintained their position in Division 3 of the Birmingham League and Wormelow who consolidated their place in Division 3 of the Worcester league.

CHAPTER XII

In Memoriam

Whilst it is not possible to mention every cricketer who has sadly passed away, especially in view of the period of time that this book covers, there are some who the authors feel deserve a special mention because of their influence on cricket in the County.

Bert Howells died on the 1st October 2008 after suffering a long illness. He was 81. He was born at Fawley Court near Brockhampton and was a keen footballer in his early life. He was also a Vice President of Hereford United Football Club for many years. After the Second World War Bert joined Brockhampton Cricket Club, eventually becoming club captain and chairman. He served the club faithfully for over 60 years finally becoming club umpire and assistant to the groundsman, a job which he enjoyed immensely. Bert was also a much-valued member of the Herefordshire Umpires Association; he was a true old-fashioned gentleman and will be missed by Herefordshire Cricket.

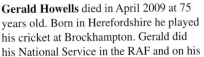

Gerald Howells died in April 2009 at 75 years old. Born in Herefordshire he played his cricket at Brockhampton. Gerald did his National Service in the RAF and on his return he married Jean his life-long wife. She died just a few weeks before him. Jean was a tremendous support to Gerald and Brockhampton CC where she was the scorer for many years and also helped out with the cricket teas and they both enjoyed the social aspect of the club. Gerald played cricket into his late 60s and was a stalwart of the club, always ready to help out with improvements as he and Jean did when helping to build the new clubhouse in 2003.

Ken Pole was educated at Hereford High School and played cricket for the school. When he left school he played a major part in the running of the Y.M.C.A. Cricket Club. When he retired from playing Ken became an umpire and played an active part in the Hereford Umpires Association. Ken died in 2007.

Harry Miles was a founder member of the Hereford Umpires Association. He was a long time umpire for the Hereford City Sports Club and also officiated in three Prudential ICC World Cup qualifying matches in 1978. Harry died a well-respected member of the cricketing fraternity.

Phil Noakes played cricket for the Hereford police, later becoming an umpire. A member of the Hereford Umpires Association he rose to become the umpires training officer and secretary. Phil died in a car accident in 1995 whilst delivering umpiring exam papers to Edgbaston.

A photograph, of the late **Ivan Bishop**, on holiday with his wife Gladys. Ivan gave valuable service to the Hereford Evening League and the Hereford Umpires Association. When he retired from all cricketing administrative duties, he and his wife took a well-earned holiday.

Fred Wooding was an avid follower of Leominster Cricket Club and was a regular spectator at the Grange.
He was buried just yards from the Grange in the priory graveyard. and his love of the game is depicted on his unusual headstone.

Phillip Powell was a Canon Frome school governor, Parish Counsellor and was on the local village hall committee. He was a representative of the National Footpath Association. He received an MBE for his service to the British Legion for over 60 years. He was a devotee of cricket, was secretary of Canon Frome Cricket Club for 22 years and continued with his task of mowing the outfield for over 30 years. He died in 2007 aged 86.

J.S. Arkwright (*standing, left*) was influential in Herefordshire cricket from the beginning of the 19th century when the family purchased Hampton Court, until the middle of the 20th after they had moved to Kinsham Court.

Noel Lewis was a schoolmaster who loved his cricket. When he left college he spent one year at Goodrich before he was appointed headmaster at Little Dewchurch primary school where he stayed for nine years. During his time at Little Dewchurch he was the opening quick bowler and captain of the local village cricket team. He moved on to become headmaster of Much Birch School where he continued to coach cricket, staying at the school until his retirement in 1982. Noel died in 2005 at the age of 78.

Noel started his cricketing career early, playing for his college team (see below).

Back row left to right: J. Nuttall, H.L. Watkins, T.U. Buckthought, D.T. Williams, W. Morgan, I. Thomas, W, L, Evans.
Middle row left to right: J. Evans, R.J. Gill, J. M. Tatchell. (captain). H.T. Sebire, R.D. Jones.
Sat in front far left is Noel Lewis; the other two players in the front row are unknown.

Dave Evans died in 1997 at the age of 65, he was probably one of the best wicket keepers the county has produced in the last 50 years. Dave was one of the game's real characters and played regularly up to his death. In his long career he played for Hereford, Bulmers, Burghill & Tillington and MEB in the evening league. During his early career his son Adrian recalled as a child going to watch his father playing for Old Hill in the Birmingham league.

Elaine Lamputt died in 2009 after a long illness. Elaine was the scorer and team manager for the Lamputt XI in the 1950s.

Mike Hughes died in 2009 at the very young age of 50. Mike played his cricket for Hay on Wye, Golden Valley and Dorstone, and was also a valued member of the Burghill & Tillington touring squad.

John Taylor of Eastnor cricket club died suddenly in March 2009 aged 58 years just before the printing of this book was completed. John was a friendly yet very competitive cricketer who played the game in the correct spirit. He was a very important member of Eastnor Cricket Club having been secretary of the club for some forty years and helped organise their many tours. Jim Sandford his friend and team mate along with many other members of the club will miss him greatly. John can be seen on page 127 collecting a trophy with Jim.

Jean Howells died in March 2009 only a month after her husband Gerald (see page 147). She was the scorer at Brockhampton for many years and was never slow in coming forward to help with any task in the club.

Rob Staite joined Hereford city sports club as a young teenager, he was a very enthusiastic quick bowler and improved his game over the years until he became the club captain. He approached the captaincy with total commitment. Rob was a well-liked person and was always a very approachable and sociable cricketer.

Rob sadly died of cancer aged 35. His family have donated 'The Rob Staite Memorial Trophy' to be presented annually to the person who has given outstanding support to cricket in Herefordshire.

Peter Pedlingham of Colwall CC died suddenly at the age of 69 in May 2009. Peter was a fine cricketer who played in the same team as Henry Horton in the 1960s. He had been associated with Colwall for more than half a century and will be greatly missed.

Derek Evans died in May 2009 after a long illness but has left a legacy of wonderful photographs; he can be seen on the Lamputt anniversary dinner photo on page 54, in the front row on the far left.

It is tragic that, in the time it took to produce this book, so many people have died. This chapter demonstrates the reason for writing the book: so these cricketing people and their achievements can be remembered.

Amendments and corrections
to
Cricket in Herefordshire in the 20th Century.

As part of the research for the above book, the writers interviewed well in excess of 100 former local cricketers over a period in excess of two years, in addition to carrying out research in the county archives and local reference library. Several hundred names had to be dealt with.

Many photographs of a bygone age were produced, some regrettably without the names of the players. It was inevitable that there would be some omissions and inaccuracies as a direct result of the passage of time and some amendments and alterations are dealt with overleaf.

2008 proved to be a difficult year for batsmen to concentrate on the game because they were reading 'Cricket in Herefordshire in the 20th century'!

Page	*Details of amendments and additions*
4	The Bringsty youngster in the photo is Oliver Andrews
18	The photograph is of Alan Roberts not Alan Richards
19	A. Ian (Tanner) Davies is Alan (Tanner) Davies
19	Flint & Cook Marches League was formed in 1992
28	The first Ross Single Wicket Competition was won by Cecil Young
30	The Bringsty 1957 team should read John Sears, not Jim
37	The Ediswan 1950s team name should read E.J. Moon not Ernie Ridger
38	Painters Syd Catley not Caffles and Les Campbell not Gambles.
39	Wyevale is mid 1950s not 1950.
40	Gas Board mid 1950s, missing Dennis Barlow
45	The name in the Saracens Head 1987 is Eric Pritchard not Eddie
51	YMCA 2nd right seated Cliff Roese.
70	Lads Club 1980. Ann Smith made all the sweaters and was a lady 2nd left stood Bernard Halfpenny, Far right stood Barry Halfpenny.
73	Melting Team back row should read Alec Carter not J. Carter
75	The name in the Front row Centre of the National Westminster Bank team photo is Richard Head, not D. Heale
76	The unknown lady in the Ross 1976 photo is Sue Newton the wife of Mark Newton the Worcestershire County Cricket Club chief executive.
82	Paul Notley scored 35000 runs in his Ross career
83	Paul Notley was Captain of Ross Nondescripts.
121	The unknown name in the Kington 1960 team back row first left is John Prater
134	In the Kingsland 1961 photo the Umpire on the right is Percy Pudge and on his left is Cliff Davies
137	The Shobdon Teal Trio should read, Matthew, Terry (Father) and Andrew
141	In the 1950 Leominster team the correct name is Jack Bemand not John Beaman
151	The name on the front row first left in the Moreton and Lyde photo is Peter Harrison
153	Harry Pudge is front centre on the Canon Frome 1970s photo
154	On the Canon Frome 1980 photo back row first left is Gerald Blandford, second from the right is Phil Hunt and front row far right is Bill Pearce. John Evans from Canon Frome is not deceased as stated, but regrettably It was John Evans from Bromyard who has sadly passed away.

165   Burley Gate 1955/56 Roly Howells.

176   Nine rows up from the left should read Ernie Mansell not Ernie Morgan.

183   In the Ross Grammar School 1940 the correct name is Roy Pittaway not Pittenway

185   Additional names for the Ledbury Grammar School 1948. Back row far right is Brian Law (scorer). On his left is Bob Turner and front row far right is Geoff Wickham

187   Herefordshire under 18s 1962 not 1958.

200   Burghill & Tillington correct name is Nick Phelps not Phillips

201   Hereford City Sports Club Bryan Smith not Brian

207   Norman Davies was associated with Ross not Leominster

Sources & References

Hereford Times

Hereford Journal

Hereford Evening News

Hereford Society Magazine

Ross Recorder

Ross Gazette

Daily Telegraph

Old Photographs of Ross On Wye (T.Rigby & A. Sutton)

Herefordshire County Cricket Club annual handbooks

Village Cricket by Patrick Murphy

Cricket Grounds by William A Powell

Marches League Handbooks

Hereford and District League Handbooks

Hereford Evening League Handbooks

Cricket in Herefordshire in the 20th Century (Ken Hook & Frank Bennett)

Hereford Library

Hereford Bulletin

The Peter Manders Collection

Index of Teams, Leagues & Organisations

Index of names

Name	Page(s)
Steele Rev	124
Stephens David	26
Sterry Fred	98
Sterry Mike	36,128
Steward Martin	65
Stewart Ian	104
Stobbs M	117
Stock Angela	55
Stonyer H E	22,140
Stooke Hill & Co	24
Strange Terry	119
Streeton B R	13
Strickland Mr	63
Styles Chris	128
Suddes J	99
Surridge Stuart	25
Sutch Screaming Lord	47
Swancott Simon	77
Swivell Dick	109
Sykes Peter	15,66,74,83,108
Symmonds Amy	19,106
Symmonds Neville	91,92
Symonds Brian	27,44
Symonds G	65
Symonds Jeremy	27,44,130
Symonds Margaret	38
Symonds Neville	52
Symonds Robbie	108
Symonds Ted	38
Taylor Andy	53
Taylor Brian	125
Taylor Eddie	79
Taylor John	41,127,150
Taylor Ken	21
Taylor Lee	70
Taylor Mr	95
Taylor Ron	79
Teague Alan	80,113
Teale Andrew	121
Teale Matthew	121
Teale Terry	121
Terai Mustapha	32
Terry J	78
Terry J T	61
Terry John	129,145
Thirkle Bob	129
Thomas	62
Thomas Adrian	86
Thomas Bill	100
Thomas Brian	80
Thomas D	111
Thomas Fred	132
Thomas J P L	60
Thomas M	99
Thomas Mr	60
Thomas O D	60
Thomas Rev W.R	131
Thomas Rob	100
Thomas Tudor	63
Thompson M	43
Thornycroft C G M	78
Thornycroft Lt. Col. C M	90,92
Thornycroft G M	90
Thurston R	99
Thurtle Hati	55
Thwaites Richie	83
Tidmarsh Jean	119
Tidmarsh Mike	119,124
Tilley Luke	14
Tinton Bill	116
Tipping Brian	80
Tipton Dick	120
Tolley F J	123
Tomkins J	122
Tooze Ollie	77
Toplis E G	59
Topping J B	133
Tozer P F W	59
Treagus Val	125
Trenchard Clive	78
Trounson Kate	67
Trueman Freddie	36,106
Tumelty Joe	66
Turner Bill	121
Turner David	62
Turner Glenn	102
Tutchenor Brian	130
Twigg D	112
Twyman T A	17
Underwood Derek	44
Vale J N F	123
Vaughan R H	59
Veale P K	60
Verdin J	117
Vernalls J	122
Verry Dave	42,107,108
Verry Duncan	68,108
Verry S D	72
Vicaridge Emlyn	144
Vickress Bob	115
Vickress Jim	115
Wade Joe	24,85
Wade John	125
Wade Robert	85
Wadelin Jack	110
Wadelin Neil	110
Walcott Murray	106
Waldren Shaun	108
Walker Jonny	143
Wall Alan	120
Wall B	103
Wall L J	96
Walsh Tim	129,145
Ward G	99
Ward Hugh	80
Wardell A	82
Warden Robin	19,28
Wargen Roy	46,105,106,108,143
Wargent D	90
Waring Andy	108
Warley George	59,60,77
Warley John	59,60
Warley Roger	142
Warner P F	16
Warwick Bruno	54
Warwick Gabriel	54,66
Warwick Sebastian	8,54
Warwick Theresa	54
Watkin Gareth	68
Watkins A	13
Watkins Andy	143
Watkins B	82
Watkins Maurice	104
Watkins Rob	90
Watkins S G	72
Watkins Steve	8,86
Watkins T	99
Watkins Thomas	116
Watson	62
Watson Ken	90,119
Watson W F	123
Watts M	43
Weaver Andrew	94
Weaver Josh	70
Weaver Mr (Burley Gate)	119
Weaver V	103
Webb R	96
Webley H	123
Wells David	28
West Don	90,95,96
West Edward	65
West Stan	95,96
Weston Ashley	68
Weston Charles	69
Weston Len	85
Wetson Bill	98,99
Wetson Ernie	99
Wetson Jack	99
Wetson John	99
Wheeler Ben	146
Wheeler Julian	86
Wheldon F	17
Whitaker Sandra	55
Whitbread Tim	101
White B	110
White Bernice	53,54
White Johnny	53,54
Whitlow J P	17
Whittaker Andrew	55
Whittaker Dick	129
Whittaker George	36,128,129
Whittaker Jack	109,129
Whittaker P	43
Whittaker T	122
Wilden Mr	95
Wilkins G	99
Wilkinson Miss	138
Willetts Duncan	74
William Jack	40
Williams A	103
Williams Andy	32
Williams Bert	79
Williams Brothers	115
Williams C	99,122
Williams Cyril	87
Williams E	105
Williams Eric	139
Williams Gabby	67
Williams Geoff	65
Williams Georgette	67
Williams Jack	100
Williams Keith	80
Williams Ken	87
Williams Kevin	106
Williams Mick	77
Williams Mr	135
Williams Norman	32,113
Williams Oliver	66
Williams R	78
Williams R B	62
Williams Robin	106
Williams Roy	85
Williams S	70
Williams Selwyn	83
Williams Steve	8
Williams T L	62
Willis John	32
Willmott D	43
Wilson G	17
Wilson Peter	86
Wilton Simon	130
Wiltshire Jim	84
Winchester Eric	43
Winter Ada	127
Winter Ted	127
Withers Dale	66
Withers Noel	101
Witts Gordon	65
Wobley Colin	88
Wolfendale Tom	146
Wolstenholme Arthur	63
Wood G	82
Wood Geoff	82,87
Wood J	90
Wood John	86
Wood Mr. (Withington)	116
Wood Richard	68
Wood Roy	82
Wooding Fred	148
Woodpower Dr	90
Woodriffe Pat	54
Woodriffe Ted	34,53,54
Woodward J	95
Woodward Joe	59
Woolridge Sandy	142
Worthing Dennis	31,42
Wragg David	116
Wragg Harry	25,116
Wragg L	116
Wragg T	116
Wright Paul	48
Wyevern Flooring	24
Wyman Gerald	104
Yapp G	65
Yarnold Hugo	90
Yarwood Nigel	77,78
Yemm Chris	104
Yemm David	104
Yemm John	104
Yemm Percy	104
Yemm Sylvia	104
Yeomans Carl	93
York Susannah	32
Young Cecil	152
Young Royston	152
Young Stan	113